BUILD YOUR
DIGITAL
MARKETING
STRATEGY

THE MINDSETS AND METHODS OF BUSINESSES
THAT DOMINATE THEIR SECTORS ONLINE

STEVE BRENNAN

RETHINK PRESS

First published in Great Britain 2018
by Rethink Press (www.rethinkpress.com)

© Copyright Steve Brennan

Contents

Preface

This book is a practical guide to help you make sense of digital. It will be of particular help if you have some marketing resource in house, and it will be helpful if you hire in support from digital agencies or contractors too. It will guide you through building your digital strategy, organising your team to deliver it, building great digital assets to support your marketing, and developing great daily routines that enable you to dominate your sector.

Before we get into the nitty-gritty, I'm going to use this preface to tell you a little about myself and why I decided to share these methods in a book. The book itself is factual and can be read in full, or dipped into when you want a refresher on a particular aspect of your digital strategy. This preface is the only part about me. After this it's all about you.

I've worked in digital marketing for almost twenty years. Most of that time I have been CEO of Bespoke, a digital agency based in the north of England, serving clients in the north and in London. In early 2017 I ran three strategy workshops in a week for relatively high-profile clients whose senior staff all shared feelings of overwhelm or confusion about their digital marketing. They made statements in the sessions that told me they had deep concerns beyond the questions they'd brought to the workshop – 'I feel vulnerable, we're falling behind', 'I feel my staff know I'm out of my depth on this', 'we just don't know where we should be focusing our time.'

All three workshops took the same course. The clients booked on the premise of specific digital challenges they faced – they'd booked social media, digital strategy and content planning workshops. But when the day came, they presented broader issues and eventually began using quite emotional language. I recognised their anxieties from previous workshops I'd run, and from workshops that colleagues had run and then discussed with me. I remembered our team saying that on occasion clients had used our workshops like counselling sessions. Running three workshops in a row enabled me to join the dots, and I realised if these people felt disoriented by digital, others must too.

On the spur of the moment I committed to getting this book written and published within a year. I imagined it would simply be a case of 'brain dumping' the concepts from the workshops and accelerator programmes our agency runs. But when I started it didn't go as I had expected. The process began to have impact for me personally, and I quickly realised that this was the first time in twenty years I had stopped to contemplate the knowledge my colleagues and I had accumulated over that time, both in terms of what makes digital teams and campaigns work, and of what makes them fall short, as so many do.

Then stranger things started happening. I began to realise why I do what I do. As I made more and more notes, and sketched out ideas and a structure for the book, I saw patterns that reminded me of things I had done in my childhood. I realised I could draw a line from what I did as a kid in my bedroom, back in the eighties and nineties, directly to running digital strategy workshops and accelerators, and to running a digital agency.

I always felt my teenage years were less conventional than those of most of my school friends. Dad was an alcoholic and left home when I was 10, and Mum became the breadwinner. At that age my younger brother and I ate a lot of sandwiches, so the bread she won didn't last too long. We were happy enough, so not being well off didn't feel like a big deal to us, and, of course, we didn't actually know any different. But we had to be resourceful to some degree.

I took a job delivering newspapers so I could have pocket money. I took as many shifts as I could, and right through my high school years I delivered papers mornings, nights and weekends. I loved unbundling the hot-off-the press papers, seeing night turn into day. I loved knowing the news first, too. I could go to school and tell people about the latest football transfers. For some reason Chris Waddle to Marseille for £4.5m in 1989 is one I remember vividly – it felt exciting knowing about it before everyone else at school.

I didn't mind inky fingers and I liked being the first kid up on our estate, arriving at school exercised and up to speed on what was going on in the world. I also loved the people side. It felt good knowing all the grown-ups on the estate and seeing them heading off to work. I was curious about what each of their jobs was like. I came to recognise different types of people, and different types of cars and vans, and I recognised which kind of person read which kind of newspaper. The man with the green Jaguar who took the *Telegraph* gave me £5 each Christmas, which I couldn't believe. The painter and decorator with the transit van gave me £1 but talked to me more. On some basic level I was becoming aware of demographics, without realising.

My weekly wage of £10.50 was spent on going to the football (my local team Preston North End was a two-mile walk from my house) or on one of my regular walks into town to buy the latest vinyl records. I'd been fascinated by music from primary school age and loved my little record player as a six-year-old. I only had a few ex-jukebox seven-inch singles by The Police, Eddy Grant and Howard Jones that we'd picked up for ten pence at the local market. Now, with that small weekly income, I could buy my own twelve-inch singles and LPs. I could build my own collection like my dad's but with my own identity. The first LP I bought was a glossy-sleeved double album by Frankie Goes To Hollywood. I loved the music of course, but the artwork was great too and I'd sit reading every detail of who had been involved in each record as I listened to it. I liked to try to unravel the puzzle of what had gone into making each one.

By thirteen I was curious about taking things further and placed an ad in a national football magazine to sell football programmes. A friend and I had been buying them in cheap bundles from a stall at the local market. We produced a catalogue and listed them for sale individually at a higher price. A small-scale enterprise but an enterprise nevertheless and a taste of what it was like to be in business.

By sixteen I'd begun writing and designing my own football magazines, cutting and pasting them punk-fanzine-style at home. I recruited a couple of friends and we pieced together a magazine to sell at matches. The initial 200 copies sold out in no time and

I immediately wanted to do another to see how much we could increase that number. We grew circulation to 2,500 and won a bunch of national awards before I wrapped the magazine up a few years later. Looking back I can see we grew by testing different designs, pricing, features and methods of selling, and with each tweak we learned a bit more. We were doing user testing and A/B testing but didn't realise it.

I continued publishing magazines as a sideline while studying media and communication at university in Birmingham, and then at twenty-one joined the world of full-time work as a designer for our local newspaper. At the same time I took a weekend job as a DJ in a nightclub in the city centre. I saw no connection until I sat down to write this book, but now realise I'd gone from a school kid delivering newspapers and buying records to a young adult making newspapers and magazines, and playing out records to an audience.

DJ-ing entailed a weekly residency and competition from other nightclubs was intense. If you got the music policy wrong, or the pricing wrong, the audience gradually migrated elsewhere. We talked about it all the time, and tweaked and adjusted hoping to grow our share of the audience. With the music, there were new records each week. We DJs had to judge what would be likely to work and then test it with the audience. Will they react well to White Stripes directly after LCD Soundsystem? Can this new band called the Arctic Monkeys go straight in at peak time without clearing the floor? When's the right moment to drop Teenage Kicks? We paid real attention to detail on audience reaction, and doubled our numbers as competitors came and went.

I saw everything as something that could be improved with a strategic approach. If there was an audience, and you could engage them, then you could delight them more and more as you learned more about them. But you had to listen, observe and understand them. You couldn't be half-hearted with it – you had to be fully committed. They had to be able to see you were doing it for them. And you could never relax because there was always another new competitor just around the corner.

In my mid twenties, while working as a designer and DJ, I became curious about something I kept hearing about called 'the internet'. I wasn't completely sure what it was and nobody I knew seemed to be sure either. But, apparently, we'd be able to publish content for the whole world to see from our own bedrooms at very little cost. We'd be able to change and update it at any time, and include photographs, sound and maybe even video. I learned how to build websites at home in the late nineties, saw what was possible and promptly quit my day job to go all in on this new way of communicating.

There was no such phrase as 'digital agency' or 'digital marketing' when two friends and I founded our agency in 2001. People just wanted to get online to find out what it was all about (or in some cases they didn't because they felt it would never take off). There was no social media, no broadband. When we went to pitch to clients we connected via their phone line, which meant their phone was engaged while we browsed websites during our pitch to them. We advertised in a small section for internet companies in *Yellow Pages*. We were early adopters serving early adopters, not realising how things would scale up for us and for so many of our new customers in the years that followed.

In the near two decades since, our agency has worked with hundreds of businesses to build and run digital strategies that have enabled them to use digital channels to grow. Most have turnovers of £5m to £100m but we have also helped plenty to go from zero to £1m+ online to become established firms. This book shares the patterns around what is usually occurring within a business's digital strategy and digital campaigns when it is scaling up and dominating its sector online. There are some things that are almost always in place and these are explained over the pages that follow.

I'm in my forties now and my mission has become simpler – to help people build great businesses, careers and lives on the back of digital and the opportunities it brings. I've seen plenty of people's lives transformed by the strategies they've implemented online. I've seen people build businesses that have sold for millions of pounds, and I've worked with established businesses to help them embrace digital and dominate their sectors online. It's the most satisfying thing to see people succeed, and I wrote this book so that you have a chance to adopt the mindset and methods of those who have been the biggest winners over my first twenty years in digital marketing.

We're in an age now where digital is dominant, yet it remains a discipline that is still evolving and has not yet fully matured. The land grab is still on, as it were. The businesses that build the best digital strategies now, while it's still possible to win market share easily, will dominate their sectors in the 2020s and the 2030s. You're a step ahead of some of your competitors because you've chosen to read a book like this. But remember there are no rewards for those who just read – the rewards go to those who are the quickest and the most successful in implementing what they have read. Think of it as a race between you and your competitors, and use this book as your secret weapon to make sure you win that race.

Introduction
Mindset

The five mindsets
• • • • • • • • • • • • • •

O ver two decades I've worked with more than 1,000 business owners, marketing directors and marketing managers to help them organise their digital strategies. I work with some in group workshops and some in one-to-one sessions but I always go deep on their business and its online goals. I now find I can often gauge within fifteen or twenty minutes how successful that person or team is going to be with their digital marketing over the next year or two.

That's because I've seen over these twenty years that so much comes down to mindset. The successful businesses – the ones that accelerate their growth the most and in some cases result in dominating their sectors online – bring the 'Strategy Mindset' to their digital marketing, just as they would to other parts of their business.

Businesses that find they're often playing catch-up bring different mindsets. Some like to have a hand in lots of different digital channels in the hope that some work (the 'Lottery Mindset'). Others like to outsource their marketing and keep it at arm's length (the 'Agency Mindset'). Others like to hire one or two people in house, or a couple of freelancers, and hope they're able to deliver better results than competitors that way (the 'DIY Mindset').

As the digital sector has matured, it is increasingly the business with the Strategy Mindset that dominates its sector online. But the digital land grab is still in progress, which means there are still plenty of opportunities for businesses to adopt a strategic approach with digital and take market share while it is still relatively cheap and easy to do so in most sectors.

Every year more businesses mature towards strategic approaches to digital marketing and in time the digital space as a whole will shift that way. Competition in each sector online gets stronger every year and it becomes increasingly difficult to unseat businesses that have established large market share – partly because a history of success is one of the things Google values. The only sensible tactic is to be among the first in a sector to master digital marketing and accumulate market share while it is easy to do so.

In this section, we'll look at the five mindsets businesses bring to their digital marketing. We'll also consider why most businesses move slowly and gradually towards a strategic approach. We've found that awareness of the different marketing mindsets helps people to understand why they are performing as they are online.

But first let's take a moment to consider why so many businesses don't yet have a fully developed, mature, strategic approach to digital marketing. If you feel your business or the business you work for doesn't have a solid and complete long-term digital strategy in place yet, don't worry. Most businesses don't – although that will soon change.

There are three reasons why most businesses don't yet have fully developed digital strategies:

1. **Digital marketing isn't a mature discipline yet.** It's an area that has developed at extraordinary speed and is still rapidly evolving. Most businesses weren't using social media or video channels even ten years ago. Also, because these are new disciplines, most don't have digital marketing as a core skill in their business either. So it's to be expected that most businesses haven't yet established what best-practice digital marketing looks like.

2. **Anybody can present as a digital marketing expert.** The barrier to entry is low. Formal qualifications aren't needed and those that are available are easy to get. Compare this with other professional services, such as finance or law, where years of study and examination are needed to become a practitioner. So by definition, even when businesses have hired in experts or staff, the chance of whoever has been hired offering the very best practice is not particularly high.

3. **They don't know where to start.** So often,
this is how those who attend our workshops
and accelerators feel. They talk of the whole
topic being overwhelming for them. They've
heard conflicting advice and have had some
poor experiences. So digital ceases to become
something they fully commit to. There are areas
of their business they understand deeply so
they focus on those instead, rather than dealing
with building a long-term digital marketing
strategy.

These factors discourage people from applying the
Strategy Mindset to their digital marketing when actually a strategic approach is exactly what's required.
They need a mindset where:

- their blueprint for digital success has been
thoroughly researched

- tactics have been chosen based on expert insights
and experience

- a great team has been assembled

- the right assets have been produced to support
that team

- the complete strategy exists in a published
document everybody can understand

Our agency typically meets with businesses that have
turnovers in the £5m to £100m range and are mostly

well established. Yet our experience is that fewer than one in five of the businesses we engage with bring this structured and strategic approach to their digital marketing.

But without exception, when we meet with businesses that have evolved to this level, they routinely achieve online goals and in many cases are able to dominate their sectors online. They report feeling relaxed and confident about the online side of their business. To them it's just another part of their business that is well organised and that they know is set up to run well for many years to come. This book exists to give *you* the opportunity to achieve that same level of stability, predictability and satisfaction from your business's digital marketing strategy.

Now let's take a look at the five mindsets businesses typically bring to their digital marketing (see Figure 1). Many businesses take a linear route through them for reasons that will become clear as we learn about each one. But there are exceptions – more experienced and astute business people skip steps to get to a Strategy Mindset more quickly. Usually this only occurs when a particularly knowledgeable digital marketer who has learned from experience is involved in the business. Hopefully this book will provide a shortcut to that stage for you.

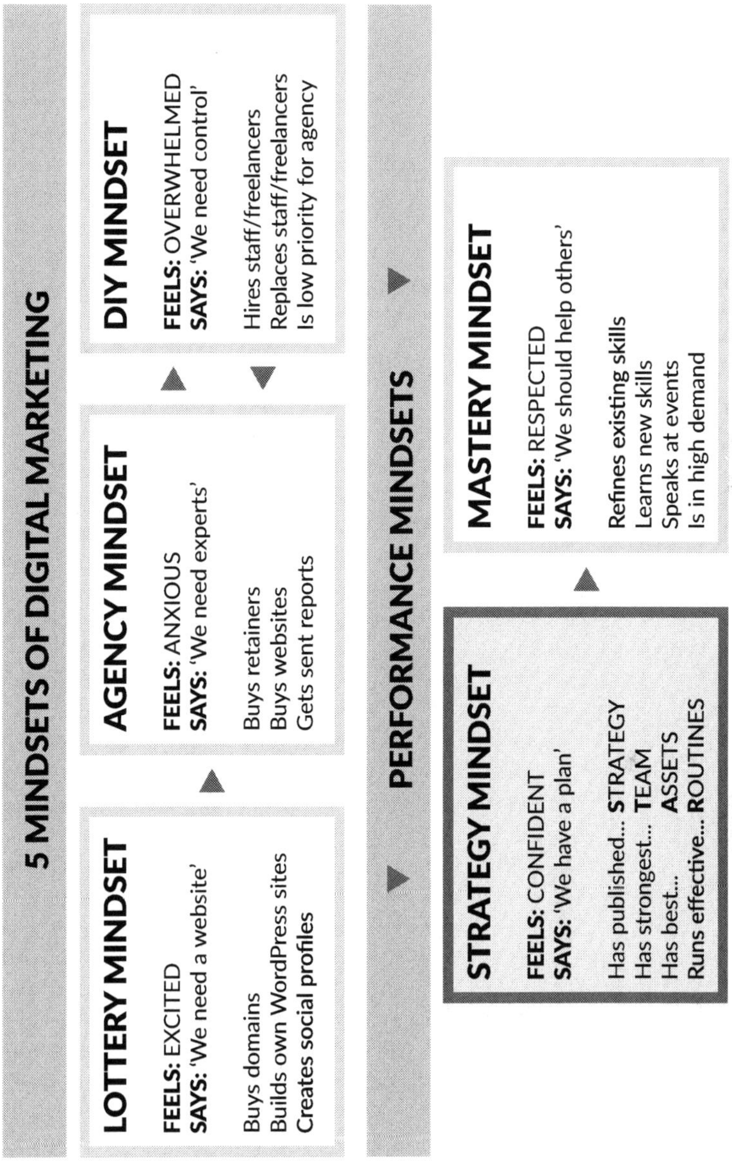

5 MINDSETS OF DIGITAL MARKETING

LOTTERY MINDSET

FEELS: EXCITED
SAYS: 'We need a website'

Buys domains
Builds own WordPress sites
Creates social profiles

AGENCY MINDSET

FEELS: ANXIOUS
SAYS: 'We need experts'

Buys retainers
Buys websites
Gets sent reports

DIY MINDSET

FEELS: OVERWHELMED
SAYS: 'We need control'

Hires staff/freelancers
Replaces staff/freelancers
Is low priority for agency

PERFORMANCE MINDSETS

STRATEGY MINDSET

FEELS: CONFIDENT
SAYS: 'We have a plan'

Has published... **STRATEGY**
Has strongest... **TEAM**
Has best... **ASSETS**
Runs effective... **ROUTINES**

MASTERY MINDSET

FEELS: RESPECTED
SAYS: 'We should help others'

Refines existing skills
Learns new skills
Speaks at events
Is in high demand

Figure 1 Digital marketing mindsets

We'll run through each of the five mindsets in a little more detail and maybe you can identify which of the five your business has had previously and which it has today.

The Lottery Mindset

The Lottery Mindset is all about wanting to be in the game. You can't win if you don't have a ticket. So those with a Lottery Mindset put up a website before fully researching their customers' pain points or fully establishing how they are going to position themselves in the market. They feel good registering social handles and domain names without knowing whether they are needed or not. They create a video – any video – because their competitor has one.

When we started our digital agency back in 2001, everybody who contacted us had a Lottery Mindset. They would phone us and say, 'I keep hearing about this internet thing and I feel like I should have a website. Can you help?' They had to have a Lottery Mindset back then of course. We'd expect them to, because simply having their business visible online felt like a step in the right direction and, as with anything new, there is some fear of missing out too.

But today, almost two decades later, many still present this mentality. They want to spend some money on X or Y because they've heard it's going to be big, or because they've heard somebody else is doing it. Equally, they are closed to certain digital tactics because they didn't work once before, or because they've heard somebody say they don't work.

Lottery Mindsets are about rolling the dice and taking some risks to have a chance of winning. Occasionally those with the Lottery Mindset get lucky and win for a while, but in the end the competitor with the thoroughly researched strategic approach comes along and steals big pieces of the pie. When that starts to happen, there's recognition that the Lottery Mindset isn't going to work in the long term and a different approach is then sought.

The Agency Mindset

When a business's first attempts at digital marketing fail to deliver and its owners see competitors gaining ground, their first reaction is to look around for help. But normally the full range of skills and experience needed to run great digital campaigns doesn't exist within the business itself. So the natural next step is to look externally and the most obvious ports of call are the local digital agencies that appear in web searches for 'websites', 'digital marketing', 'SEO company' and so on.

This is a leap of faith and in some cases appointing an agency means committing funds beyond what a business might have considered spending on digital marketing before. But often the business is committing those funds when it isn't experienced enough to select or brief an agency properly. So, while it feels a more secure approach, a significant element of chance remains. Most businesses don't get their first agency appointment right and many take several attempts to find the agency partner that is the right two-way match.

But the Agency Mindset is a step up because it at least provides the possibility of good outcomes for a period of time, and it means there has been some acceptance that digital is important to the business. In 'Hiring Digital Agencies' in Part Two, we'll learn what makes client–agency relationships succeed or fail, but in short the client needs to be a priority for the agency and there has to be regular face-to-face communication for reporting on specific goals.

On appointing an agency, there is often a feel-good factor and optimism about what can be achieved. There may even be monthly visits to the agency's smart offices and that feels good for a while too. Irrespective of how good or bad the results are, there may be further changes in approach to come as the business realises it hasn't tried all the options yet. It has no benchmark for what is good and what is bad, and eventually it begins to get itchy feet again about its approach.

The DIY Mindset
A business accumulates some elements of under-standing about digital marketing as it works with agencies, contractors and freelancers, and as it hears

about new developments in digital. If the business can see competitors getting ahead online, it naturally becomes anxious and that anxiety, combined with some degree of understanding of digital, leads it towards believing that the best approach might be to organise its digital marketing itself.

Couple this dynamic with the fact that many smaller businesses have a mindset that is focused more on cost than opportunity, and the outsourcing approach can come under real scrutiny. An agency retainer normally costs several thousand pounds a month so there is inevitably the lightbulb moment within the business of 'Shouldn't we just hire somebody and do all this in house?' There begins the DIY Mindset.

The DIY Mindset has a chance to work when implemented openly with an already successful agency partner, or with specialist help from some other trusted partner to help organise the new team. It tends to work only when a business is large enough to support a skilled marketing team in house. But small businesses don't normally have the experience to hire, train, organise or retain the best digital marketers internally, and equally the best digital marketers don't normally want to work in small digital teams.

So the DIY Mindset rarely results in an immediate uplift in results because the spread of skills an agency brings is replaced with the narrower skills of one or two individuals. The agency is often kept on in some capacity or is called back to help when this approach has failed, but the business is often no longer a priority for the agency because it has other clients who are committed to them for the long term. On the upside, the business has tried a new approach and learned a lot from it. It may not realise it, but it is now closer to understanding what a thorough and balanced long-term approach to digital marketing looks like.

The Strategy Mindset

The Strategy Mindset is when a business's approach to digital marketing has matured. Decision making is no longer going to be based on whims but on research and expertise. The business is going to make sure that the experts it has to deliver its campaigns are better than those of its competitors. And it is going to invest in great digital assets to support its marketing in the long term too.

The first step in the Strategy Mindset is to assess:

- what the business wants to achieve

- what its customers need from it

- how it should position itself to deal with those needs

- what its competitors are currently doing

There is normally a full review of tactics and bold decisions are taken on which ones should be used and which discarded. The digital strategy is published in the same way as the broader business plan.

The business establishes who needs to be around the table each month when results are reported and tactics are reviewed, to ensure the certainty of outcomes. Normally this involves both internal and external stakeholders, all of whom are experts in their area. Leadership and ownership are clear, and all parties working for the business are fully invested in building strong long-term relationships.

Businesses that dominate their sectors online almost always have an established Strategy Mindset. Often these are larger corporates that have a similar mindset across other parts of their business. But small businesses can dominate their sectors online and can even rival corporates when they bring a corporate-style Strategy Mindset to their digital marketing. The Strategy Mindset is when digital teams start to feel empowered, and when businesses sense certainty and predictability about the results they are going to achieve. This is the place to be and this book will show you how to adopt a Strategy Mindset for your own digital marketing.

The Mastery Mindset

There is a fifth and final mindset that is a level beyond the Strategy Mindset and can only be accessed by those who've practised the Strategy Mindset for some years. It's called the 'Mastery Mindset' and fewer than one in ten marketers we meet through our digital agency work have it.

The Mastery Mindset occurs when a Strategy Mindset is so embedded in a business that it has become second nature. The digital team achieves predictable success almost on autopilot. It knows how to run different types of campaign, even for a new product or service, and can report back to senior management with certainty on what results will be possible for whatever the future marketing objectives happen to be.

In organisations with a Mastery Mindset, the weekly activity tends to be about keeping skills up to date by following training programmes, attending events, planning new campaigns or hiring in specific expertise to help in areas where a skills or resource need is identified or predicted. Leaders of teams with a Mastery Mindset are invited to speak at events or train others. They're respected in their field.

The best digital marketers aspire to work for businesses with a Mastery Mindset because they have the chance to learn best practice first hand, they can more easily contribute to the success of the organisation and they can progress their own careers as a result. A business of any size can achieve the Mastery Mindset in time but it can only do so once it has practised the Strategy Mindset successfully for several years. So the Strategy Mindset is the route to success for most marketers and for most small businesses.

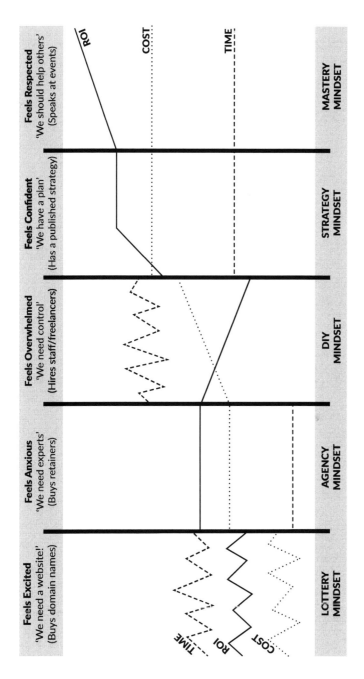

Figure 2 Outcome of the five mindsets

When we run workshops and accelerators, we talk to delegates about the five mindsets of digital marketing. They can normally identify where on the scale they currently are and where they have been in the past. We look at Figure 2 and they recognise how their mindset influences the outcomes they achieve from their online marketing, and also the amount of time and money they spend on it.

Next, we're going to consider what it looks like to bring the Strategy Mindset to your business's digital marketing. But before we do that, let's consider where else people might adopt the Strategy Mindset in life – these are principles that apply far beyond digital marketing.

Developing a Strategy Mindset

So, if adopting a Strategy Mindset is the route towards predictability and success in digital marketing, what does it look like when a business is taking a strategic approach? Four elements are always in place:

1. **Strategy.** There's the strategy itself of course. This is based on insight and thorough research (as opposed to whims or trial and error). There's clarity and certainty about which tactics are likely to be appropriate to achieve the goals and which are not. The strategy exists as a published document that everybody involved refers to.

2. **Team.** The team delivering the strategy is as strong as, or stronger than, competitors' teams.

Everybody has appropriate skill and experience, and is motivated to achieve the business goals. Digital teams are often a mix of in-house staff and experts from agencies, or contractors. But they're set up and behave as one team, with a leader keeping everyone on track with the published strategy.

3. **Assets.** The strategy and team can only succeed when there are great digital assets to support the campaigns. Businesses that apply the Strategy Mindset to their digital marketing make sure they have better websites than their competitors, better branding, better social channels, better image libraries, better marketing automation and so on.

4. **Routines.** With the three foundations in place, strategy-based marketers then develop daily, weekly and monthly marketing routines that bring their strategies to life. They set up repeatable processes that make it easy to publish regular content that speaks to their customers' pain points, and they refine and improve continually, based on the results their routines deliver for them.

Combined, the four elements are referred to as the 'S-T-A-R (Strategy, Team, Assets and Routines) formula'. The most successful marketing teams in each sector are well developed in all four areas. If a business is only well developed in one or two areas, it's likely to be playing catch-up on those competitors more and more over time.

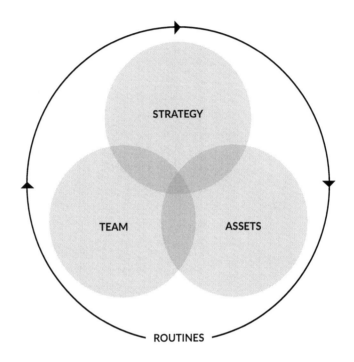

Figure 3 The S-T-A-R formula

Figure 3 illustrates how the first three elements in the S-T-A-R formula combine to give a business a solid foundation for its digital marketing. Then the routines, the fourth element, run in cycles to get as much return as possible on the investment the business has made in developing that strong foundation – the digital strategy, team and assets.

In our day-to-day digital agency work, we often meet prospects and clients who are frustrated because they have invested lots of time and money in their digital marketing but find they are still falling behind competitors. Normally, it is simply that they have made good progress with some of the four elements but not with others. The business that is dominating the sector is well developed in all four areas – it has a fully developed Strategy Mindset. Once a business understands this distinction, it becomes much easier for it to address its approach to digital and move towards high performance itself.

Where digital is concerned, the four elements of the Strategy Mindset are usually adopted by the businesses that dominate online in each sector. But as we've established, digital is not a fully developed discipline yet. As it matures over time, more and more businesses will adopt a strategic approach and become fully developed in their approach to digital.

But while digital may be a new discipline, in other areas of life best-practice approaches are well established. In some cases, they've been tried and tested over decades. So surely the Strategy Mindset must be the established approach in these more mature areas of life? Let's take a look at three other disciplines, away from digital, that are mature and where achieving a particular outcome is considered vital, and see how the Strategy Mindset is applied in those.

Professional sport
Professional sportspeople have an objective to achieve the very best result possible. In football, for

example, managers lose their jobs quickly if results aren't being achieved. Clubs lose millions of pounds when competitors overtake them. In British football, Manchester City have established themselves as title-winners after decades of minimal success by adopting a Strategy Mindset with its four elements as follows:

1. **Strategy**. The club publishes a strategy that covers its recruitment, playing style and planned investment in facilities. It researches competitors thoroughly, including competitors from other countries. For individual matches there is a published strategy and the printed document is shared by everybody on the manager's bench during the game.

2. **Team**. The club does everything it can to assemble the best team on and off the field. It set a mission to bring in the world's best manager and boardroom staff who had achieved success at other big European clubs. It invests millions – more than anybody else – to make sure it has the best players for delivering on match days.

3. **Assets**. For a football club, the players are assets – the club buys and trades them. Manchester City also invests so it can have the best training and academy facilities of any competitor. It knows that a great strategy and great team need the best assets to dominate. So it provides its team with

the best assets, and this has already resulted in lots of success.

4. **Routines.** With the three foundations in place, the club then goes about daily and weekly routines of researching competitors, training and practising, and then on match days it delivers its strategy while electronically monitoring literally every step each player takes on the pitch. It reviews and refines performances this way and, by constantly improving, it eventually began to win trophies and to dominate.

The corporate world

In the corporate world, leaders are accountable to shareholders. The consequences of not achieving required results can see senior staff losing their jobs. In some circumstances, directors can be prosecuted for mismanagement or for misleading markets. Results become critical so the organisation adopts the Strategy Mindset and puts the four elements in place as follows:

1. **Strategy.** Public companies are legally bound to inform markets of their plans. So strategies are established and shared in AGMs, through staff meetings and through published documents. Individual departments have their own strategies too, such as those for hiring or marketing. Business plans are based on analyses of market trends and competitor activity.

2. **Team**. Corporates invest heavily in assembling the best teams. Some have in-house departments dedicated to hiring and HR functions. For key roles, headhunters are employed to get the best people. Corporates understand that they need to have the best people to succeed.

3. **Assets**. Corporates aim to invest in the best locations, working environments, equipment and the best marketing collateral they possibly can so their teams have the best chance to succeed. They understand their strategies and that teams can't succeed if they aren't backed by great assets.

4. **Routines**. Patterns of daily, weekly and monthly activity are established and often documented in staff handbooks, or as standard operating procedures. Key performance indicators are owned by named individuals and there are face-to-face meetings at set intervals to report on progress.

The military

The consequences of not delivering intended outcomes in military operations can obviously be more extreme than in any other area of life. Military law applies and malpractice can result in a court-martial being convened – responsibility at its highest. Because their outcomes are so critical, the military bring an intense Strategy Mindset to their operations and the four elements are always evident, as follows:

1. **Strategy.** Missions and campaigns are approached with detailed strategies based on intelligence on the environment they expect to encounter, and the risks and opportunities associated with them. There is clarity on tactics among teams and clear leadership structures to make sure campaigns remain on track with the agreed strategy.

2. **Team.** The military invest heavily in recruitment advertising and put huge focus on training drills to make sure they have the best people available when campaigns begin. It's only possible to move up the hierarchy by accumulating experience and showing a track record of success.

3. **Assets.** The military know a great team can only deliver campaigns successfully if it has great assets to support its efforts. So governments allocate billions to developing military hardware to equip their teams with the best resources possible for their campaigns.

4. **Routines.** Daily, weekly and monthly drills occur during both training and campaigns. Personnel are clear on standards that are expected and outcomes that must be achieved. There are regular inspections and reports to make sure teams maintain standards.

	Professional Sport	Corporate World	The Military
STRATEGY	Strategy document used during game based on research into competitor	Strategy published in business plan, markets notified of plans	Campaign strategy published, with clear tactics and insight on risks
TEAM	Best possible coaches and competitors hired, clear leadership	Best execs headhunted to run in-house teams to get best from everybody	Large numbers recruited, train intensively to have best people when needed
ASSETS	Invest in best possible facilities/equipment for training and matchday	Invest in best possible facilities/marketing to deliver on business plan	Invest in best possible equipment/resources for military campaigns
ROUTINES	Electronic monitoring, refinements made based on findings	Regular reporting-in and reflection; adapt to improve where needed	Routines of drills/checks maintain standards. Campaign adapts if needed.

Figure 4 The Strategy Mindset in other areas of life

So, while the digital sector may not yet be fully developed, in other areas of life that are well developed and where results are vital, the four elements of the Strategy Mindset are always evident. It follows then that, if we apply similar levels of thoroughness to our digital marketing, we create the opportunity to achieve similar levels of success and predictability of results.

Now that we have some understanding of what it means to operate with the Strategy Mindset, we'll take a deep dive into each of the four elements of it. We'll look at how they apply where digital marketing is concerned when a business is adopting the Strategy Mindset to scale up and dominate its sector online.

PART ONE
STRATEGY

Build Your Strategy

In this section, I outline a methodology for creating a strong and effective digital marketing strategy that can be published and used by everybody in our digital team. We'll learn which components are always present in a great digital marketing strategy document, and also about the research and planning that goes into creating the strategy document.

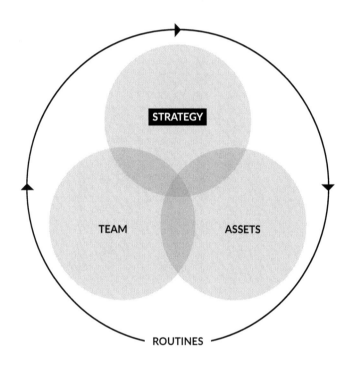

Figure 5 The S-T-A-R formula

Let's start by considering what a 'strategy' actually is. An obvious starting point is to take a look at how the *Oxford English Dictionary* defines the word: 'A plan of action designed to achieve a long-term or overall aim'.

We already know that a strategy is a plan of action but notice that the dictionary definition also refers to 'a long-term or overall aim'. So a strategy is about moving us from a current situation to a different future situation (see Figure 6). In digital marketing, that might be a straightforward growth aim or it could be more elaborate, perhaps moving us into a new market, launching a new product or service, or repositioning us to appeal to a different audience.

Figure 6 Moving to a new situation with a strategy

Either way, we're more likely to be successful on our journey to our future situation if we're clear what our current situation is. So understanding and communicating both our current situation and our intended future situation is something we will have to do if our strategy is to have a chance of being successful.

Achieving buy-in
· · · · · · · · · · · · · ·

Before we begin researching our strategy, there are things we can do that help achieve buy-in from our team as the process progresses. Here are five things to consider:

1. **Share the purpose.** We may have a clear understanding of why we are about to embark on new campaigns but that doesn't mean that all our digital team understand our grand plans. Being super-clear on the 'why' behind the campaigns we're about to embark on means colleagues can become excited and eager to be involved.

2. **Gauge the response.** The project leader's job isn't just about clear communication; it's also about careful active listening. Potential team members might be excited about our plans but not quite clear about their purpose. They may even feel the goals we are proposing are unrealistic. We need to know how they feel so we can make sure our strategy document contains all the information they need to understand the journey we are about to go on. This way they can feel involved.

3. **Involve key stakeholders.** There may be people we have in mind to help us deliver our strategy – perhaps senior marketers we have in-house or key staff from our agency partner. They'll deliver more effectively if they feel they've been involved in the formation of the strategy from the outset,

so that they feel ownership rather than it being imposed on them. If we brief them early, we may also be able to incorporate their views or ideas into the strategy.

4. **Deal with resistance.** For the most genuine of reasons, we may encounter resistance before we even begin executing our strategy. Colleagues may feel proposed budgets could be better spent elsewhere, proposed goals are unrealistic, or simply that our plans look like too much hard work for them personally. Objections need to be nipped in the bud before we start implementing, and our team needs to be formed exclusively of people who are on board from the outset if it's to deliver on its goals.

5. **Reward ownership.** Often, when there is a new project on the horizon, some colleagues are genuinely interested and recognise it as an opportunity for themselves. We'll need people on board who will push hard towards our goals. If we reward those who show willing ahead of a project getting under way, we show others our project is important to the organisation and that there are benefits for those who drive us towards success.

We will only achieve buy-in at any stage of course with a strong and effective strategy document, so let's take a deeper look at each of the five areas that our strategy document needs to address.

1.1

Know Your Customer

Marketing connects when it triggers emotional responses in people. That response might be a curiosity to learn more, a feeling of wanting to be part of something, a desire to engage, or a straightforward decision to buy a particular product or service.

At its most effective, marketing creates a strong emotional response where our fellow humans love our content so much that they become avid fans, following and remaining loyal to our brand, sharing our content for us and, if our content is strong enough, combining to make it go viral.

A good marketing team, therefore, has to be able to identify what will generate a strong emotional response in its target customer. And the only way that can be achieved is by getting to know our customer on a deep level.

Picture one person

We have the best chance of creating a strong emotional response when our marketing appears to speak directly and personally to the recipient. It's easier to create campaigns that achieve that when we're clear on who the individual is that we want a response from.

Marketing fails to connect when a company talks about itself, rather than showing the customer it understands them. As it happens, digital agencies are among the worst offenders where talking about themselves is concerned, but again that isn't so surprising given that digital is not a fully developed sector yet. They will get better at marketing themselves in time.

For our purposes, we need to visualise, hear and almost see the world through the eyes of the one person who is the exact target for our product or service. Maybe we know a good example of that person already? Being able to name an individual always helps, and by considering an example target buyer this way we have a chance to make a strong connection with people.

This method of visualising a single individual is well established in other fields. Newsreaders are trained to picture one person and that helps them look the camera in the eye in a genuine and personal way. Some people apply the same principle when they give speeches in public. The technique works just as well when we want to communicate authentically through marketing.

Get inside their head
Three questions help us shift from our own mindset to our customer's mindset. Working through these questions in order takes us deeper into what our target buyer has on their mind.

1. What are all the problems our customer might have? (When we start to work deeply through this question, we can often list fifty or more.)

2. When they wake at 4am, what is on their mind? (What are they anxious about? What are the deep worries they have as individuals? What is the main thing they want or need?)

3. What's really going on? (It may not just be a need for our service, but perhaps a desire to appear credible or successful, or a deeper fear about the progress of their career or their business.)

I've always found it interesting to ask questions more than once in different ways. When I meet with clients, I ask what they're looking to achieve and what challenges they have. It's rarely the first answer that reveals the deepest issue. But if I ask two or three times, in different ways, it tends not to take too much effort for the real issues to come to the surface.

By way of example, people normally book sessions with me on the premise that they have a particular idea in mind to achieve more leads or sales. But when we meet, there are much deeper concerns about their approach to digital as a whole. Sometimes they feel their issue is hiring the right people for their team, or allocating the right budgets. Sometimes there is an even bigger issue, like they have lost confidence in a colleague or provider. It doesn't come out with the first question and it wouldn't be the first guess you would make at what was important to them. So we have to go deeper and ask probing questions to fully understand what problems our target buyer is looking to solve.

Create a buyer profile

A buyer profile might also be referred to as a 'user persona' or 'customer avatar'. Various templates for these are available online (see Figure 7) but many fall short for digital campaigns because they don't nail down how the target buyer consumes digital content or deal with commercial factors such as whether they are able to approve budgets and make buying decisions themselves. If we don't have those details, we can't plan and target our marketing campaigns effectively.

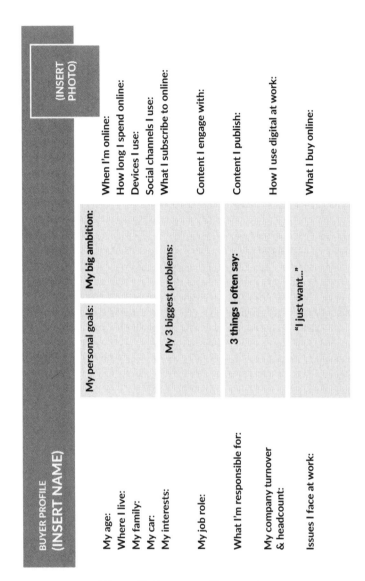

Figure 7 Buyer profile template

To produce a useful buyer profile for a digital campaign, we take a sheet of A4 or A3 paper and, using it in its landscape orientation, divide it into three columns as follows:

1. **Personal.** In this first column, we begin to profile the target buyer. We try to be as specific as possible. Our aim is to identify a good target buyer, not a range of people, so our answers should describe one person:

   - What age is our best possible customer?

   - Where might they live?

   - Are they single, married, with children, etc.?

   - What car would they drive?

   - What are their interests and hobbies?

   - What job do they do?

   - What are they responsible for?

   - What is the turnover and headcount of their company?

   - What issues do they face at work?

2. **Needs.** In the second column, we are dealing less with specifics and more with understanding our target buyer's needs. We include a photograph now, and give them a name so we can start to visualise them:

- What do they look like? (Use a Google image search to find somebody who matches the profile in column one).

- What personal goals do they have?

- What is their biggest ambition in life?

- What are their three biggest problems or worries?

- In a one-hour meeting, what three things would they often say?

- If they could just have one thing happen, what would it be?

3. **Digital.** In the third column, we need to understand how our target buyer behaves in a digital environment. This will help us make better decisions as we decide on tactics later in this process. So we ask:

- When are they online each day?

- How long do they spend online each day?

- What devices do they use each day?

- Which social channels do they use?

- What do they subscribe to online (newsletters, YouTube channels, etc.)?

- What types of content do they engage with most?

- Do they publish any of their own content online?

- What do they use digital for at work?
- How frequently do they buy or order online?

Working through this process helps establish a picture of the person our marketing is going to target. Publishing this in our strategy helps our delivery team consistently create content that appeals directly to our target buyer. It's important of course that all our marketing connects with the person we have profiled – if we're inconsistent, our communication won't feel genuine to them.

Stress-test the profile

Once we have our buyer profile in place and we're familiar with the process, it's possible to take things a step further by stress-testing our profile with real customers. These may be people we've worked with previously or people we feel match the target buyer profile. Some ways to stress-test the buyer profile we've created are to:

- **Conduct online surveys.** With Google Docs, Survey Monkey or a Twitter Poll, we can quickly gauge responses on simple key questions. For example, we can offer multiple choice options on what problems our target buyers are looking to solve and we can ask questions about the digital channels our target buyer uses.

- **Run test events.** It's relatively cheap and easy to run a two-hour breakfast event on a topic we feel is important to our target. The event should be based on the big, deep issues they have. If we've pitched it well, we'll get good attendance, and an interactive session means we hear our target customer speak openly on the issues in question.

- **Openly ask.** If we know some people who match our target profile, it can work simply to ask them to describe what their biggest issues are. Doing so has multiple benefits. Aside from generating valuable insight, customers are often grateful to be asked to share their views. It shows them there is a genuine desire to give them what they want and need.

Once our buyer profile has been stress-tested and we're happy it's good to go into our strategy document, we're ready to move on to the next section and get to know our competitor, too.

1.2

Know Your Competitors

To scale up and dominate a sector online means doing better than one's competitors. A business can only achieve this when it is clear as to who its real competitors are. So it must have visibility on what they are doing online and what results they are likely to be getting. With that understanding it has a benchmark to beat, and tactics can be planned accordingly.

With an Agency Mindset or a DIY Mindset, a business might simply decide to allocate £100,000 to its digital marketing for the year, because that's more than last year so it should be enough for this year. But if its competitor has decided to allocate more budget and spends it wisely, the competitor will dominate again and increase their market share further.

Businesses with a Strategy Mindset invest time in developing deep insight into their competitors' thinking and activity. They profile them and watch how their approach develops over time. It's possible, by monitoring a competitor's activity, to reverse engineer and identify the decisions made in their marketing meetings. Once we have that level of insight, we're at a real advantage if we're looking to scale up and increase our own market share.

Our competitors might not be those we immediately identify. Small businesses sometimes struggle to shift focus from long-standing competitors when the bigger threats are actually from more agile newcomers who can solve our customers' problems in new or different ways.

Hoover thought its competitor was Electrolux, then found out it was Dyson; HMV thought its competitor was Our Price, then found out it was Apple; and Borders thought its competitor was Waterstones before learning the hard way that it was actually Amazon.

Throughout history, businesses are blindsided by newcomers or established competitors who quickly reposition to compete directly for the attention of their customers. So our strategy must also include thorough research on our competition so that our digital team can be clear as to who and what we are up against, and what we need to do to outperform them.

Conducting a simple digital audit

Audits come in different shapes and sizes but there are some things they must always achieve: they must leave us with thorough insights into how our activity differs from that of our competitors, and the impact those differences are having on our results. Some common initial questions in a digital audit are as follows:

- Are we sure we have identified the right competitors to compare ourselves against?

- Does their marketing suggest they have the same business objective as us?

- Do they appear to be targeting the same buyer profile as us?

- What key phrases do they repeatedly include in their website code and social content?

- Which digital channels are they active on and which have they chosen to ignore?

There are many more specific tests that should be carried out, some manual and some automated. Remember that businesses with the Strategy Mindset base decisions on research not whims, so regular auditing like this is one way to collect information.

When our audit is done, it's useful to summarise the main quantifiable results in a table so we can see at a glance which competitors are strong in which areas and how they compare with us. We need the detail of the full report in our strategy document, but the table is valuable for quick reference and a great benchmarking tool if it's updated every few months (see Figure 8).

	Pages	Page Speed Score	Mobile Friendly Score	Domain Authority	Social Posts in Last Month	Videos in Last Month	Website Type
Our Web Presence	177	81	71	31	14	12	Laravel
Competitor #1	68	48	55	17	42	33	WordPress
Competitor #2	356	64	31	22	3	0	WordPress
Competitor #3	111	57	43	41	51	19	CraftCMS

Figure 8 Simple digital audit summary report

Website audits

It's also important to audit our websites and those of our competitors. Websites are key assets that differentiate the high performers from those who are always playing catch-up. They're where transactions take place and enquiries are made. Some aspects that are assessed in a website audit are as follows:

Site architecture. How many pages are indexed in Google? We can easily check what pages Google has indexed for a business by typing site:domainname. com into the search bar. The same way, we can also see at a glance what keywords the business is choosing because its page titles give hints as to its search engine optimisation (SEO) strategy. Professional auditors use tools that do far more detailed site architecture analyses but this is always an interesting aspect to quickly review.

Domain authority. The Open Site Explorer tool at Moz.com gives a domain authority score. This is Moz's own score and is not used by Google. But it gives an indication of how much authority Google will give a website based on the number and quality of links to it from other websites. It shows the best links and a spam score – which we want to be low of course.

Page speed. Google's Page Speed Insights tool gives a score for the speed of a website on desktop and mobile devices. Speed influences how well search engines rank a website and also how many visitors go on to buy or enquire. So speed has a direct impact on results. An audit should compare speeds and, in Google's tool, scores of around eighty or more represent success.

Calls to action. For a website to perform, its content has to include good calls to action (CTAs). These may be forms where the visitor can submit an enquiry or request a quote, or they may be something bigger like an 'add to basket' feature on a shop, or a 'request a brochure' feature on a lead generation website. Noting the differences between CTAs across competitors gives insight into their marketing aims.

Mobile compatibility. A well-built, responsive website will perform well across all mobile, tablet and desktop screen sizes. If coded properly, a website should be readable by screen readers and, if it incorporates Accelerated Mobile Pages (AMP), Google will recognise and reward this. Google now ranks websites based on their mobile performance ahead of any other criterion.

Organic search. Organic search rankings aren't quite as valuable as they used to be because much of the top of the search results screen is now given over to paid for or local listings. But they are still significant. There are many tools to track search rankings and compare them over time against those of competitors. Auditors usually work across at least twenty phrases because fluctuations in one or two can give a false impression of overall performance. Most websites win traffic from at least 1,000 different key phrases so the performance of one or two doesn't usually reveal much.

Conversion rate. This is the percentage of visitors who go on to buy or enquire. Often the visitors a business needs are already arriving at its website but because something is not quite right they don't go on to buy or enquire. If a conversion rate is 3% and increases to 4.5%, that's a 50% increase, so leads or sales go up 50% without any extra visitors. We can only see our own conversion rate and it's good practice to track it and work to improve it incrementally.

Search Console. Google's Search Console provides reports on our website's performance, but not on those of our competitors. It tells us about broken links, problems indexing certain pages, site map quality and so on. Apart from the reports it provides, we can use it to change settings for our website, for example around structured data, XML sitemaps and pagination preferences.

Content audits

Some areas that are often investigated while auditing content include the following:

Content pillars. Can we identify what content pillars our competitors are using? In other words, are there key themes and messages repeated throughout their content? What themes and phrases recur? Do they show understanding of the target buyer's biggest issues? Are they consistent across all channels? Do they change over time? Is the content presented in a rich, valuable way that both Google and the target buyer will appreciate?

Readability. Written content on the web has to be succinct and crisp. The eye should be able to scan a page and understand the key message. We view the web at speed, with a short attention span and often while scrolling. Readable text should be broken up with bold headings, bulleted lists and illustrations. Tools are available online to check text for readability – for example, the Flesch Reading Ease test. Do our competitors write better for the web than we do?

7/11/4. In 2011, Google published its theory that prospects need to consume at least 7 hours of content over 11 separate touchpoints across 4 channels before they reach the 'zero moment of truth' (ZMOT) when they are ready to buy from us (see Figure 9). That means 11 interactions in total over 4 different channels. In real life, the exact numbers are not these in every case, but the concept is useful. To achieve 7/11/4, a business must have a coordinated mix of content across different channels that the target customer can find easily. Which digital channels are our competitors active on and which are they ignoring?

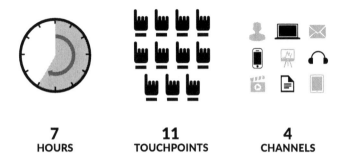

Figure 9 Google's 7/11/4 concept

Social media. The 7/11/4 principle means social channels are key to any digital marketing strategy, so a content audit should be asking questions about these too. Does the business have a presence on Facebook, YouTube, Instagram, Twitter, Pinterest, LinkedIn or others? Are profiles branded well? Do the social media handles match? Have the pages been professionally optimised? How many posts on each in the last thirty days? How much engagement on each in the last thirty days? How many followers on each? What percentage of posts contain images or video? What percentage are new content and how much is recycled?

Paid search. Is the business running paid search campaigns? If so, for what products, how often and in what position? Can we tell if the ads are being professionally managed (i.e. does copy follow best practice?) or might the business be wasting some budget on paid search? Is it using remarketing? Is it showing in paid positions on social channels too?

Video. It's increasingly rare for businesses to be able to scale up and dominate online if they aren't publishing regular video content. Done well, video builds trust and can quickly show that a business understands its customer's biggest issues. So is the business publishing regular video content? Is it professionally shot? Is it short form or long form? Is it published on social channels and is the audience engaging with it?

Forecasting the future

At the beginning of this section, we saw how businesses can be blindsided when they are too focused on current or past competitors. So once we've researched the current competitor landscape, we should also consider what might happen next in our sector, in order to pre-empt changes.

Some questions we might ask are as follows:

- Is ours a mature, well-established market?
- How likely is it to be disrupted by new products or cheaper solutions?
- How likely is it to become saturated?
- Is demand for our product or service likely to rise or fall?
- Is the value of our product or service likely to rise or fall?
- Are any competitors showing signs of repositioning?

- Might our target customer use a different kind of supplier in the future?

- How might broader economic factors affect our market as a whole?

- What is the size of our market and who currently has what share?

- What is the most profitable business within our market?

- What new products or services might emerge in our market?

- Which competitors are most likely to grow or contract?

Giving consideration to who our competitors are, where they currently are and where they are likely to be in the future makes us more likely to build a strategy that will work over its full life. All markets evolve over time and businesses that have adopted the Strategy Mindset are alive to that and monitor changes in their markets on an ongoing basis.

1.3

Define Your Niche

Businesses dominate their sectors when they offer exactly what their target buyer is looking for. The target buyer can tell straightaway that they are the supplier they are looking for. In an environment where an alternative is just a click away, a clear and simple offering to a prospect is key to attracting their interest.

To maintain that interest, our offering has to be compelling too. If we consider that Google's 7/11/4 concept is also at work, meaning a customer needs to engage with us in several different ways before they are ready to buy, the offering probably has to be memorable too. And all this is more of a challenge online than anywhere else because our prospect's attention span there is at its shortest.

So our strategy has to be clear on ways to:

- differentiate
- win against strong competitors
- stand out
- be memorable

The outcome has to be that, when our target customer finds us, they immediately relax and feel they have found exactly what they were looking for – the answer to their problem.

How to niche
• • • • • • • • • • • •

It wasn't possible to define our niche until now because it can only be done with the deep knowledge of our customer and our competitor. We needed to document those aspects first and, now that we have, we can consider exactly how we can reposition ourselves given that context. To go through the niching process, we need to focus on two areas:

1. **Our customers' biggest problems.** We want to niche as much as we can towards our target customer's biggest problems – our marketing must address their pain points.

2. **Our competitors biggest weaknesses.** We want to niche as much as we can towards our competitors' biggest weaknesses – our marketing must exploit those where it can.

So, for example, we can niche by targeting our marketing towards particular sectors. Then we can build campaigns specifically for those sectors. If we couple these with exploiting a competitor's weakness – perhaps we can deliver our solution better or faster – we give ourselves a great chance of appearing as a perfect fit when prospects find us online.

Finding ways to win
• • • • • • • • • • • • • • •

Before we draw up the niche positioning statement for our strategy document, let's consider some ways businesses can find to win online within their sector. Remember digital is still an underdeveloped discipline where best practice isn't the norm, so opportunities do exist to outperform others. Eventually, these opportunities won't exist so this is the time to take steps to win market share.

In most sectors, there will be several businesses that are good at many things, so we may have to look carefully for the weaknesses of others to find ways to win. But those gaps and opportunities will exist. For example, if we're reselling somebody else's product or service, we can't make it different or better but we might be able to win by offering better payment terms, faster delivery or more efficient after-sales service.

Here are ten ways small businesses find to win online:

1. **Fastest response.** Some offer instant callbacks. This is not only convenient but also suggests there is a well-staffed office, which reassures the prospect (even if they don't want the quick callback). The option to choose a time for a callback can differentiate a business too.

2. **Best feedback.** Some businesses show that they have the best customer reviews in their sector – perhaps the most five-star reviews or the highest average. There is work in collecting these but they do build trust in prospects, and Google recognises and likes them too.

3. **Customer service.** Some businesses make it clear that there is a friendly team to speak to during the buying process and after purchase. Prospects need to see evidence of this through images or video. Visualising that there is somebody there who cares builds confidence in a brand.

4. **Delivery options.** Prospects often think through concerns about delivery as they make purchases online. Can I get it when I want it? Can I choose a date or time? Is it convenient? The company that deals with these questions and offers the best options has an edge.

5. **Payment terms.** Similarly, payment terms can cause prospects to gravitate towards one supplier over another. It may be that the price is fine but a prospect needs phased payment spread over two financial years. It's worth asking customers what payment terms work for them.

6. **Most experience.** Presenting as having the most experience of delivering a product or service de-risks a purchase for prospects, particularly if that experience is in delivering to people like them. Some businesses gain an edge by making it clear that they have more experience than others.

7. **Best pricing.** There are lots of reasons why businesses don't seek to win on price and for some it's a valid strategy. It may be that a business offers the best price only at a certain level so it attracts exactly the size of client and

orders it is looking for, but aims to be seen as expensive by those it doesn't want to attract.

8. **Trial opportunity.** A light-touch trial opportunity, such as a short strategy call, sample product or event, can help move prospects towards larger purchases. Something as simple as a free initial report or assessment, for example, can mean one business getting far more enquiries than anybody else. These have to be managed carefully of course but they give genuine prospects a chance to engage for the first time with little risk or commitment.

9. **Compelling story.** In some cases, a business develops an edge simply because it has a great story. Maybe the business has an interesting history or origin, has delivered for some huge brands, supports a great cause, or maybe the owner has an interesting backstory. Stories are a way for brands to become memorable and a competitor who has a brand with a great story has an advantage over those who don't.

10. **Free callback.** Of course, finding ways to win only works when they are known to prospects. It's no good having an offer of a free callback if it's only advertised on the contact page of a website, or free delivery options if they're only mentioned at check-out. We're fickle online and will have wandered off somewhere else if questions are left unanswered. Ways to win only become such when we shout about them.

Seven steps to finding your niche

• •

For the purposes of our strategy document, we need everybody to be clear on exactly what niche our business has created for itself. This means our marketing must have focus and be targeted directly at the buyer profile we built at the beginning of the marketing process.

A simple way to do this is to create a niche positioning statement (NPS) for the team to follow. Below is an example of a recent NPS our team developed for one of their campaigns.

1. We are...	2. We are a...
Bespoke	Digital Marketing Agency

3. We specialise in...
Helping businesses to build digital strategies
that enable them to dominate their sectors online

4. We do it for...
£5m+ professional services companies

5. When we speak to...	6. They say...
Marketing managers, marketing directors and owners	They just want to know they're doing digital better than competitors

7. They love us because...
Our team of experts works closely with them every month,
building digital assets that deliver consistent results,
and when they have a problem, we respond within an hour.

Figure 10 Niche positioning statement

For an NPS to work well, we must challenge ourselves as we fill out each of the seven statements. Here are some tips on how to build a strong statement:

1. **We are ...**
   This should be easy – it's our brand name.

2. **We are a ...**
   Hopefully we'll find this easy too – it's what type of business we are.

3. **We specialise in ...**
   Now we have to think carefully and name the outcome our target buyer wants to see. No waffle – as few words as possible to show them we specialise in solving their biggest problem. Just our core product or service as their solution – nothing else.

4. **We do it for ...**
   Now we have to show them we function for people just like them – we know their sector, their business size, their demographic, their geographical area. Whatever will make our target buyer recognise they've stumbled across the perfect match for their needs.

5. **When we speak to ...**
   Take it a step further by getting personal. Who is our individual customer? Picture that one person. Remember the buyer profile we created.

Use the job title if there is one, or some other way to identify them. Just a short sentence that pinpoints exactly the key person our marketing will connect with.

6. **They say ...**

   This is the big one – it's where we document our understanding of the biggest problem for everyone who will be involved in our marketing. Short, succinct, true. What do they say over and over, when their guard is down, when they are being open and direct about their problems? What is the core problem they are trying to solve when they search for us?

7. **They love us because ...**

   For our marketing to land, they are going to have to love us. So we fail if we can't fire off one, two, three compelling reasons to close. We'll say we solve their biggest problem while doing three other things. And those three other things will be things competitors struggle to match us on.

With this statement in our strategy, we are focused on those we are aiming at, those we are up against and the message we want to land when we deliver our marketing. We will have some good insight by this stage and so should be ready to decide on the digital marketing tactics that are likely to be effective.

1.4
Choose Your Tactics

Earlier, in the Introduction, we explored how the Strategy Mindset is applied in other areas of life and we saw how it's used in more developed sectors than digital where achieving results is critical. We looked at how the corporate world, professional sport and the military use it to help them adopt the right tactics and implement them well.

Unfortunately, most small businesses don't apply such elaborate thinking to choosing digital marketing tactics. So they waste time and budget on activity that, with a little research and planning, they could have identified was unlikely to work for them.

In this section, we'll look at how small businesses that use digital to scale up and dominate their sectors online choose the right tactics. We'll learn how their decisions are based on insight and expertise rather than whims and hearsay.

The right blend

Before we start looking at specific tactics and how we might go about selecting or refining them, let's consider what we want to end up with. In Part One we learned about Google's 7/11/4 concept, which says that a prospect needs to consume at least 7 hours of content with 11 different touchpoints across 4 different channels before they reach their zero moment of truth, when they feel ready to buy.

So we know we will need to be marketing across at least 4 channels but it will probably need to be more, especially as we are looking to achieve 11 different touchpoints or more. So our aim is always to build a blend of tactics that will deliver the appropriate experience for our customer.

Questions to ask when choosing tactics

Businesses with a less developed approach to digital marketing ask questions like these when they choose tactics:

- What other marketing could we do?

- Have you heard Instagram is supposed to do well now? Should we try that?

- SEO isn't working. Shall we start some paid search instead?

- Do you think we need to do an extra blog each month?

- When was the last time we sent an email to our customers?

With the Strategy Mindset, we're more focused and ask questions like:

- Which social channels does our customer use?

- When do they have time to engage with our content?

- How would we reach them at work and at home?

- What content would they find genuinely valuable?

- What would they want to share or engage with?

With the second set of questions, we have a sensible set of tactics that give us a good chance to make fast progress. Businesses that ask the questions in the first set go round in circles producing inefficient digital marketing while competitors with a more customer-centric approach build market share. This second group is thinking strategically.

Three steps to choosing tactics

Digital marketing is such a broad area it's rare for the same set of tactics to be the best approach for two different businesses. And we'd expect that, given that every business is aiming at a specific target customer, while competing against a specific set of competitors.

So how do we make sense of all the opportunities that are available? There are so many tactics that can be used in digital marketing that they can't all be listed in this book. A trusted and experienced digital partner would normally assist with drawing up the options. In this book, we'll work with a set of forty of the most commonly used tactics and illustrate a three-step process that helps us filter towards the most appropriate tactics for our particular strategy.

Step 1 – Where is your customer?

This first step is as much about ruling 'out' certain tactics as it is about ruling them 'in'. We're looking to identify tactics that aren't likely to match with where our customer is, nor how they like to engage with content. We need to keep a strong focus on our buyer profile as we work through this section.

Think also about our completed NPS, our buyer profile and what it is we are wanting to communicate to our target buyer. How might those messages be best shared? Do they need video explainers? Do they need some long form or downloadable content? Or short repeated messages? Or, as is often the case, a mixture of all four?

For each of the tactics, make a decision as follows:

- **In:** Our target customer would engage with the tactic and it is suited to our message.

- **Out:** This wouldn't connect with our customer or doesn't suit our message.

- **Reserve:** We're not sure, so this tactic doesn't make the cut now but remains an option for the future.

It is helpful here to rule out as many inappropriate tactics as possible so that we have stronger focus on those ones that will help our marketing. Working through the exercise will bring a certainty that will benefit us when we begin implementing our strategy. This is about drawing up a strong and well-thought-through shortlist that we can refine further later.

Consider the various channels through which your customer could find you:

In	Out	Reserve	
☐	☐	☐	YouTube
☐	☐	☐	LinkedIn
☐	☐	☐	Twitter
☐	☐	☐	Instagram
☐	☐	☐	Facebook
☐	☐	☐	Email Inbox
☐	☐	☐	Search Engines
☐	☐	☐	Websites
☐	☐	☐	Games
☐	☐	☐	Apps

Consider the content your customers engage with:

In Out Reserve

☐ ☐ ☐ Expert Advice
☐ ☐ ☐ Buyers Guides
☐ ☐ ☐ Case Studies
☐ ☐ ☐ Latest News
☐ ☐ ☐ Behind The Scenes
☐ ☐ ☐ Videos
☐ ☐ ☐ Podcasts
☐ ☐ ☐ Online Tools
☐ ☐ ☐ Authentic Stories
☐ ☐ ☐ Infographics

Consider what would make this kind of content reach your customers:

In Out Reserve

☐ ☐ ☐ SEO
☐ ☐ ☐ Paid Search
☐ ☐ ☐ Paid Social
☐ ☐ ☐ Display Ads
☐ ☐ ☐ Remarketing
☐ ☐ ☐ Affiliate Marketing
☐ ☐ ☐ Email Campaigns
☐ ☐ ☐ Email Automation
☐ ☐ ☐ Content Marketing
☐ ☐ ☐ Guest Blog Posts

Consider what kind of optimisation would improve results along the way:

In Out Reserve

☐ ☐ ☐ Organic Search (SEO)
☐ ☐ ☐ Paid Search Optimisation
☐ ☐ ☐ Paid Social Optimisation
☐ ☐ ☐ Conversion Rate Optimisation (CRO)
☐ ☐ ☐ Email Optimisation
☐ ☐ ☐ Form Optimisation
☐ ☐ ☐ Usability Testing
☐ ☐ ☐ Page Speed Optimisation
☐ ☐ ☐ Mobile Optimisation
☐ ☐ ☐ Training & Upskilling

By comparing channels and tactics with our buyer profile, it's possible to rule some out and others in. This first step gives us an easier starting point from which to make final decisions on tactics, and it helps direct our thinking and focus towards the right options. Next we'll start to prioritise some of our shortlisted tactics above others.

Step 2 – Prioritise channels and tactics

Every business has finite resources when it comes to the people, time and budgets available for its marketing activities. But some businesses are clearer as to what is likely to work best and so focus those finite resources on the most profitable areas.

Our next step then is to filter our shortlisted tactics by working through all those we marked 'In' and identifying if there are any that might not be essential to achieving our desired outcome. For example, if our target customer is engaging with our video on YouTube and Twitter each day, is it worth running a Facebook channel too? Where does our target buyer want to engage with us?

Obviously this step requires experience and expertise so, depending on who we have available within our organisation, we might bring in a third-party specialist. There are three questions to ask for each tactic:

- Will it have a significant impact on our achieving our goals?

- Could resources be used more profitably across other tactics?

- Can we deliver the multi-channel 7/11/4 experience without the tactic?

Our aim is to create a focused strategy where we are clear on which tactics are in play and which are not. That way we run focused campaigns with appro priate resources allocated to each, and we develop deep expertise in those areas that are important to us.

The alternative to this is the scattergun approach we described at the beginning of this section whereby businesses try a little bit of everything without doing any of their digital marketing really well. In those circumstances, prospects might find us but are unlikely to follow us, subscribe to us or engage us because our marketing doesn't appear focused. Being active in a digital channel only works if we're all in and if our prospect can tell we're fully committed to them when they engage with us in it.

Step 3 – Add campaign details

Finally, with our prioritised list of channels and tactics, we need to add notes for our team on how we expect those channels to be used. So, for each, we need a note on how it will work within the campaign. Some examples of what we might record are as follows:

- **YouTube.** A thirty-second case study every week, shared via Twitter and LinkedIn.

- **Online tools.** An interactive scorecard for prospects to rate their current performance, promoted using low-cost paid advertising on Twitter and Facebook.

- **Remarketing.** Promoting a free strategy call to everybody who completes the scorecard.

- **Conversion optimisation.** Achieve a conversion rate of at least 8% from paid search traffic.

- **Email automation.** A six-email sequence with free advice and guides for every new newsletter sign-up, including an invitation for a free strategy call.

Once this process is complete, we should have a good idea of the channels, tactics and campaign types that are likely to succeed. We should also be clear which we can forget about while we implement our strategy. Our next task is to establish what work needs to be done across those tactics, who is best qualified to do it and what goals need to be established for our campaign team to work towards.

1.5
Goals And Roles

Everybody knows that if we measure something it improves. That's Pearson's Law and it's been shown to work many times over. We expose something to the surface, talk about it, think about it and make it part of the daily dialogue across our team, and that encourages everybody to influence its performance.

However, in the work we've done for clients over the years, we've seen cases where goals have sucked the life out of campaigns. That is, the campaign didn't deliver and, when we looked at why, setting the wrong goal or an unrealistic goal contributed to that failure.

When campaigns fly, teams are rallying around the goals, they believe in them and they feel the buzz of making incremental progress towards achieving them. When goals are too high or low, it's difficult for that dynamic to develop. So in this section we're going to consider what good goals look like.

What makes a good goal?

A good goal is one that:

- is realistic and achievable
- is easily measurable
- is simple for everybody to understand
- contributes to our broad business objective

In a digital strategy document there is often an overall goal, which might be a number of leads or sales for a particular campaign.

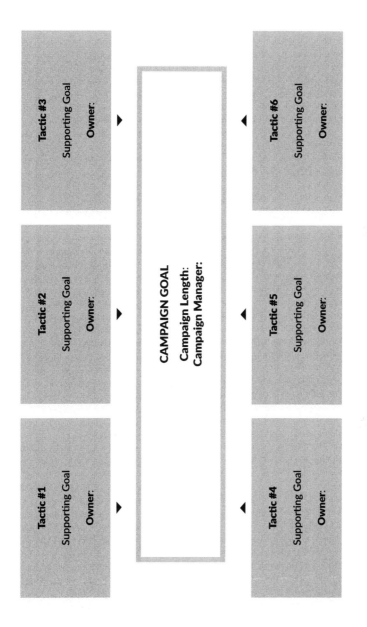

Figure 11 Supporting goals template

Usually, there are also supporting goals and the campaign team's job is to establish the best of these to ensure that the overall goal is achieved (see Figure 11). Supporting goals are owned by the relevant specialist and, when digital marketing work is coordinated well and everybody delivers, the overall goal is normally then achieved.

What bad goals look like

Bad goals – the kind that can kill campaigns – fall into three categories:

1. **Vanity goals.** For example, 'our goal is to be number one in Google for...' or 'our goal is to get our traffic up to 100,000 sessions a month'. These fail because they don't meet all the four criteria we listed above – they don't directly contribute to any broad business objective. They feed our ego maybe. But if we're obsessed with being number one for one phrase while our competitor is number two or three across 1,000 phrases, our competitor is getting way more visibility than we are and is building market share while we are not.

2. **Unrealistic goals.** A goal is unrealistic when it isn't proportionate with the resources and budget that are available to achieve it. We've often been through processes with clients to help them design strategies and campaigns, choose tactics and assign budgets. And then, when they go

ahead, they take an executive decision to reduce the planned budget or to remove one tactic. We explain that the overall goal is now unrealistic and they want to proceed regardless. The negative impact is twofold. First, the campaign is much less likely to deliver the return the client wants. Second, the campaign team feels flat, knowing it is working towards something that is unlikely to be achieved. And when a delivery team feels flat during one campaign, that is likely to transfer to some degree to future campaigns too.

3. **Unfocused goals.** Some of the businesses we have worked with over the years bring goals that shift during the strategy-building process, or which are focused on an area that isn't the key concern of the business. So the brief a business shares might be 'We have a new site and it isn't doing as well as expected so we want to grow traffic and get it converting better' or 'We want to get our PPC [pay-per-click] working better as it's a part of the business we've never got right.' In these circumstances we have to help the business to establish what it really wants to achieve. Usually, it is a quantity of leads or sales and this can be simplified to one number, which a campaign team can buy in to and rally around.

What good goals look like

Simple and clear goals are effective because teams can understand them and can be focused on them throughout every day of a campaign. Some examples of good goals we have established with clients over the years are as follows:

- Five leads per week from seven-figure turnover businesses based within one hour's travel time of our head office

- Increase monthly web sales by 30% year on year

- Fifty leads per week from directors or senior managers while halving the number of waste-of-time calls we get

- Increase quality of leads so the average order value doubles to £5,000

- Twenty-five conversations per month with small and medium-sized enterprises in the county originating from our web channels

These goals all worked because they met the four criteria. They were realistic and achievable, easily measurable, simple and easy for everybody to understand, and linked to broad business objectives.

Choosing your overall goal

We should now be able to set an overall goal for our digital marketing for the period our strategy is going to cover. Remember that a team of people are going to have to unite behind our goal if it's to be delivered successfully. Think about how simply our goal can be communicated so that our campaign team can never be unclear as to our overall objective.

For example, 'In 6 months we will have 100 rather than 75 good leads coming in every week, with a good lead being an HR manager in a UK business with £5k+ turnover.' This goal is easy for everybody involved to understand, unite behind and achieve.

A good goal will meet the four criteria discussed earlier. Everybody will be able to report quickly on it and outline the activity they will be undertaking in the week ahead to move closer to achieving it.

Supporting goals

Our next job is to decide what each of our tactics must contribute for us to achieve our overall goal. Again, we may need to bring in some specialist expertise and experience here. This is because, if we draw on past results, we can be more certain the supporting goals we put in place are realistic. Figure 12 is an example of how supporting goals would combine to deliver the overall goal described earlier.

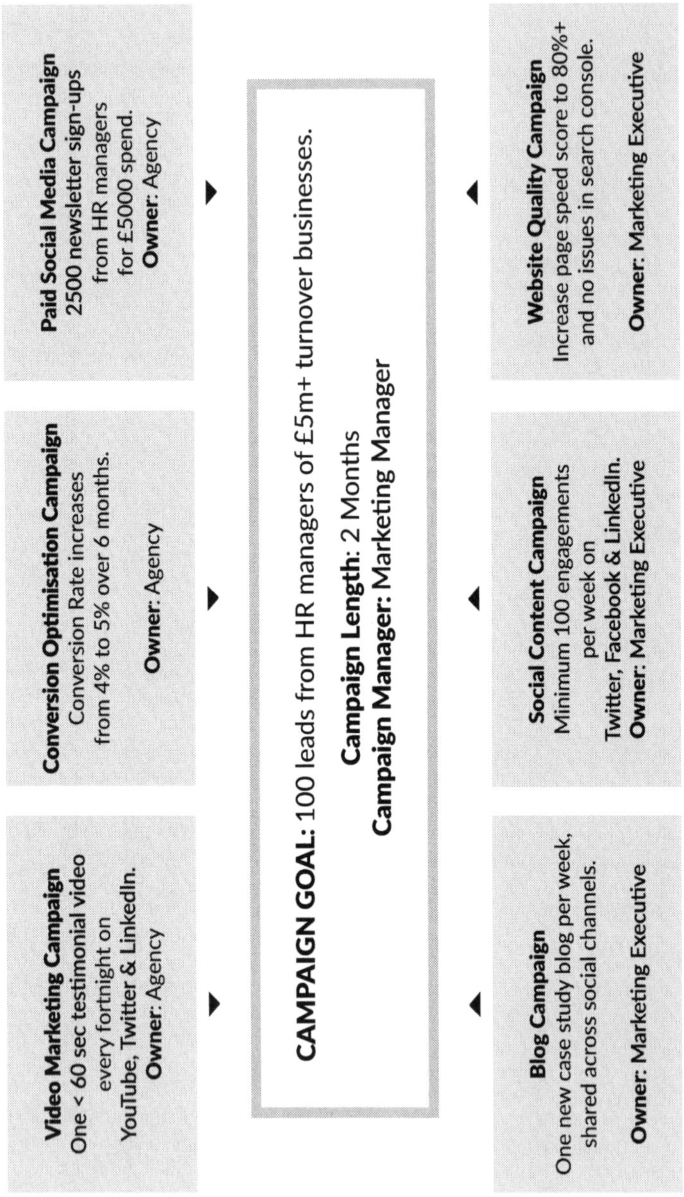

Paid Social Media Campaign
2500 newsletter sign-ups from HR managers for £5000 spend.
Owner: Agency

Website Quality Campaign
Increase page speed score to 80%+ and no issues in search console.
Owner: Marketing Executive

Conversion Optimisation Campaign
Conversion Rate increases from 4% to 5% over 6 months.
Owner: Agency

CAMPAIGN GOAL: 100 leads from HR managers of £5m+ turnover businesses.

Campaign Length: 2 Months
Campaign Manager: Marketing Manager

Social Content Campaign
Minimum 100 engagements per week on Twitter, Facebook & LinkedIn.
Owner: Marketing Executive

Video Marketing Campaign
One < 60 sec testimonial video every fortnight on YouTube, Twitter & LinkedIn.
Owner: Agency

Blog Campaign
One new case study blog per week, shared across social channels.
Owner: Marketing Executive

Figure 12 Example of six supporting goals

The spread of tactics here is enabling a 7/11/4 experience for the prospect. It's focused on just six areas. Notice how the activity in each area is clearly defined, and how the outcome from each of the six supporting goals is contributing to the campaign goal.

Ownership is key here too. Everybody works from the same strategy, but there are individual responsibilities for particular goals. If the strategy is good, the combined effect is that the overall goal is achieved. Success doesn't rely on one channel or tactic so the outcome becomes predictable and sustainable. Fluctuation in performance of one of the supporting goals is unlikely to significantly disrupt the success of the overall campaign.

We'll learn later how good tactics and goals alone aren't enough to guarantee results. We also need the right people in place and the right digital assets. But having simple and focused tactics and goals like these means we waste little time and little budget. We're doing just what needs to be done. If the other essential foundations are in place, we are highly likely to deliver on our overall goal.

Face-to-face reporting

Businesses with the Strategy Mindset have a particular approach to their reporting – namely, that they do so face to face. In high-performance environments, it's clear what each target is and who is responsible for reporting on each one. Such structures work in three ways:

- We know how each individual tactic is performing so, if necessary, we can adjust our approach based on the data that is coming back.

- Those delivering are clear on the expected outcome for their particular tactic, and everybody is clear on who is responsible for each.

- The discipline of meeting each month and reporting on progress builds focus, accountability, motivation to achieve results, and excitement and momentum when the campaign begins to deliver.

It may be tempting to skip the face-to-face meeting or check in another way. But remember that the high-growth business that's dominating your sector is meeting face to face, not glancing over a PDF report sent by email.

Pulling it all together

We've now covered the five key parts of a good digital strategy document. We've considered our customers, our competitors and how we will align our strategy to them. We've chosen our digital marketing tactics, and we've looked at how to set realistic overall goals and supporting goals.

These components form the basis of the digital strategy document our campaign team will deliver on. Next we'll look at how best to assemble the team with the best possible chance of achieving repeatable success.

STRATEGY SCORECARD

Businesses that dominate their sector online are usually strong in all four elements of the S-T-A-R formula. Score yourself on the strategy element by allocating points to each of the ten statements below, based on the following scoring system:

2 = very true, 1 = partly true, 0 = not true.

When we spend on digital marketing, we know what we'll get back.	2	1	0
When our target buyer searches online, we are the most visible supplier.	2	1	0
The leads and sales we get online are mostly from our ideal customers.	2	1	0
Our digital team understands our target buyer's motivations and pain points.	2	1	0
We know how to get the most visibility for the lowest cost online.	2	1	0
Our target buyer can find at least seven hours of content about us online.	2	1	0
We've had independent audits done on our website and marketing.	2	1	0
Our digital team are clear on which tactics won't connect with our audience.	2	1	0
Our business has a published digital strategy document for the year.	2	1	0
We know who our online competitors are and we track their online activity.	2	1	0

Add up your total to see which band your business is in:

16–20: You're working with a Strategy Mindset in the context of your strategy itself.

10–15: You've lots still to put in place before you'll scale up predictably, but you've made some progress.

0–9: This is a low score, but most businesses have low scores. Will yours be the one that steps up and improves?

Take the full test and get your business's digital strategy score at:

https://getmyscore.digital

PART TWO
TEAM

Build Your Team

Even the best strategy only succeeds when skilled and experienced people deliver it. Think of the examples earlier in this book from other areas of life. The corporate world headhunts the best people, professional sport buys and trains the best people, and the military spends heavily on recruitment and then drills its people extensively for successful campaigns.

It's no different with digital teams: the winners in each sector normally have the most skilled and experienced teams responsible for delivery. They can be teams of two or three, or twenty or thirty, but the best campaigns have the best people delivering a clear strategy, with strong leadership to unite them. See Figure 13 to remind yourself of the S-T-A-R formula.

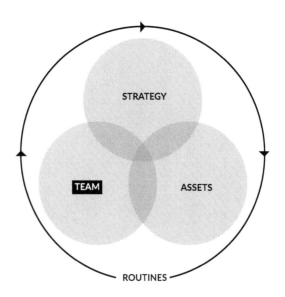

Figure 13 The S-T-A-R formula

Most businesses now have some digital expertise in house, often to undertake repeatable content work or work that requires particularly deep product knowledge. Larger firms might have a digital marketing manager. In some cases the overall marketing manager will lead the digital marketing too. External suppliers, such as agencies or experienced contractors, are normally part of the mix, bringing broader and more up-to-date skills as well as cross-sector experience.

The right allies

Remember that the digital sector has a low barrier to entry and it is not difficult for people to present as being skilled and experienced regardless of their track record. So hiring both for internal staff and external suppliers needs to be thoroughly researched and decisions carefully made.

In digital marketing, we are constantly building a footprint that Google and others will evaluate to try and understand the extent and professionalism of our organisation. Google is always looking for clues about how well developed our digital offering is. Poor work over 6 or 12 months can do plenty of damage to that footprint and it can take just as long to recover.

But it isn't just about skills and experience. We're looking for allies, people who will regard our goals as important to them personally – people who will be fully invested. Our aim is to build a team that will rally round our goals to make sure they're achieved.

What is the right mix for you?

Before we look at the three options for hiring digital marketing experts, let's consider how the nature of our business might influence our thinking on this topic.

Size of business. Smaller enterprises (six-figure and many seven-figure turnover businesses) are often best served by outsourced or contracted digital marketing experts. This is because the digital marketing requirement is rarely extensive enough to justify hiring, managing and continually training staff in house. It's also difficult for small businesses, whose core activity is not digital marketing, to attract the best marketers to come in and work for them. But higher seven-figure turnover and many eight-figure turnover businesses can often sustain full-time in-house digital marketers, normally in collaboration with agencies or contractors. These rules of thumb vary depending on how reliant the business is on digital marketing, so a business that generates most of its income from online leads or sales might hire in house sooner than a business that generates work from other channels as well.

Skills in business. While six-figure and smaller seven-figure businesses might not be able to sustain a full-time digital marketer in house, they may warrant a generalist marketer full time. When this is the case, the business needs to be clear what the extent of the marketer's digital skill and experience is before they assemble their team. For example:

- Have they led high-growth campaigns before?
- Do they have experience of hiring agencies or freelancers?
- Have they learned what to look for and what to avoid?
- How committed to the business are they?
- Are they likely to remain with it right to the end of the campaigns?
- How will they react if results aren't being hit?

Answers to these kinds of questions can help a business understand if its strategy should be led in house or by a more experienced agency or contractor. Partnering an in-house team member with the right external suppliers, with a clear leadership and reporting structure, is often the right balance.

Available resource. Once we have a good idea of the level of digital skill and experience of our in-house resources, we can consider whether or not they might be the right people to lead or help to deliver our strategy. We should also consider their likely workload and how much time existing staff will have available to deliver the digital marketing activity outlined in our strategy. If our staff are engaged in other marketing campaigns, or other objectives, assigning them to deliver our digital strategy will likely see them overstretched with goals that are not delivered. So it is not just the skill and experience we should assess in our in-house staff but also their availability to devote time and give focus to delivering our digital marketing strategy.

Figure 14 How businesses dominate their sectors online

Whatever our conclusions on our available resources, we will almost certainly need – at some point – to hire in-house staff and contractors or an agency to support them to deliver the goals in our strategy. This section looks at some of the factors that cause such hires to succeed or fail, and offers tips on questions to ask as we work through the hiring process.

2.1
A Winning Team Structure

Before we look at how to hire digital marketers, let's consider what it means to build a team. It's obviously more than just a case of hiring a group of individuals with the right sets of skills. The people we hire will only be valuable to us if they're able to collaborate effectively to deliver the goals we've set out in our strategy.

Over the years, we've seen skilled teams with good strategies fail to deliver business goals for a variety of reasons. For example, the politics at play can be such that an internal team member feels a contractor is treading on their toes, so the internal team member has some incentive for the contractor to fail. That can cause the contractor to want the internal team member out of the way too, and the result is a mess for all concerned.

So, as we build and develop our digital team, we should consider what the right blend and structure are for them to work effectively together. We need to establish clear leadership that everybody understands and accepts, irrespective of whether that leadership comes from within our business or from one of our external suppliers.

Keeping it simple

One of the most useful concepts we've observed over the years is that the businesses with the simplest team structures, with the fewest and clearest lines of communication, often perform the best. For example, where we have a small tightly knit team in house working with a small tightly knit team from an agency, with a single point of contact between the two, the scope for wasted time, misunderstanding or disagreement is significantly reduced.

With simpler structures, the likelihood is that provided we meet regularly face to face – as we would if we'd adopted the Strategy Mindset – we build strong relationships, plenty of trust and clear understanding about who is doing what and why. The result is that everybody in the team wants everybody else to succeed, simply because they grow to like and respect each other.

Conversely, where we have too many people, stakeholders and lines of communication, we increase the likelihood of misunderstanding and of some team members feeling undervalued or disconnected from the purpose of the strategy. Unhelpful politics can develop within the team. Consider Figure 15. With three stakeholders we have three lines of communication to maintain. But with four stakeholders we have six lines, with five stakeholders ten lines and with six stakeholders fifteen lines.

While most digital campaigns need several specialists involved to deliver effectively, the most successful are almost always those where the team is structured in

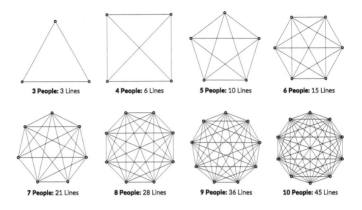

3 People: 3 Lines   **4 People:** 6 Lines   **5 People:** 10 Lines   **6 People:** 15 Lines

7 People: 21 Lines   **8 People:** 28 Lines   **9 People:** 36 Lines   **10 People:** 45 Lines

Figure 15 Multiplying lines of communication

the leanest and simplest way possible. And whatever size the team, clear understanding on who has what responsibility, who the decision makers are, and who the points of contacts are internally and externally is vital too.

Clear leadership

If the appointment of a single leader for our campaign is key to its success, how do we go about choosing that person? Should it be somebody drawn from our own staff? Should it be a contractor? Or should it be a senior team member from our digital agency partner? The answer is usually that it should be the best qualified person for the job, and where that person sits will vary depending on how fully developed our in-house digital team is.

Remember that the role of the leader is to monitor our overall goal and to make sure those responsible for delivering supporting goals are on track. So it has to be somebody who feels invested enough to take such responsibility. If we have a marketing manager or director in house, it would usually be their responsibility. If not, it might be our relationship manager or the account manager from our digital agency partner.

Our campaign leader has to be able to draw conclusions from the results of our various marketing activities as they are reported and to take decisions on potential changes accordingly. So they must have the experience and skill required to interpret results and the confidence to act on them. If somebody who has that expertise and is invested in our succeeding is in place, we have a great chance of our strategy delivering on its intended outcomes.

2.2

Hiring In-House Marketers

At the beginning of this book we looked at the five mindsets businesses can adopt when they want to use digital marketing to drive growth. The differences between the five mindsets are rarely more exposed than when businesses make decisions on whom to hire to support their digital campaigns. Hiring in-house marketers is vital in many cases but in other cases kills growth. Here we look at some of the factors that make hiring in-house marketers more likely to be successful.

Businesses with turnovers of £10m or less generally achieve the best results by combining a small number of full-time in-house marketers with a small number of contractors or an agency to simulate the breadth of up-to-date skill and experience a small internal team can't realistically deliver on its own. For many larger businesses the same is true, with the subtle difference being that the in-house team might be bigger, perhaps five to ten people rather than two to four.

The problem small businesses have to tackle is that their in-house digital teams are of a size that doesn't normally appeal as a career move to the most skilled and experienced digital marketers in their local areas. Yet, to dominate through digital, those are exactly the people we need on our team.

The best digital marketers normally want to work in larger teams or in businesses with plenty of digital expertise in house. They want regular training, peers to discuss ideas with and exposure to a variety of cutting-edge campaigns. Working in relative isolation isn't good for a career move. So, when we hire in house in a small business, we have to be clever with our hiring choices and our structuring of the external contractors and agencies around our hires if we are to build a formula that works and one that replicates the standard that our bigger corporate counterparts can achieve.

The classic mistake

The mistake we see more than any other with small businesses on a digital-driven growth path is the transition from the Agency Mindset to the DIY Mindset. The thought process when this occurs is often 'We are paying more than £3k per month to our agency. We can hire somebody for less than that and they'll be here all the time – imagine what that will do to our results!'

It's an understandable thought process but one that more often than not causes growth rates to go into decline. This happens for three reasons:

- An agency retainer provides a mix of skillsets from several consultants. These have different skills and experience and different personality types. Replacing them with an in-house hire leaves the business with just one personality type and a small subset of the skills previously accessible. An individual can't possibly deliver the same expertise that was previously provided by a team.

- The small business role often appeals to the digital marketer who – for whatever reason – hasn't been able to hold down good positions in bigger in-house teams or in digital agencies. So where a business may previously have been working with the better marketers in the area, now it is working with somebody with less skill – but they don't know it!

- Finally, the business has also inherited the task of training, nurturing and periodically replacing its hire. But, because digital marketing isn't its core expertise, it struggles to do so successfully. Instead, it enters a cycle of hiring and replacing its in-house staff every 1 to 2 years, often with a dip in the performance of its campaigns either side of those transitions.

A decision to hire in house is likely to work when it is part of a well-researched and planned strategy with appropriate support in place. In particular, it's likely to work when expertise is brought in to assist with the setting up of the new structure. It's rare for new in-house digital marketing teams to succeed when they are set up with a DIY Mindset on the whims of the owner, but more common for them to succeed when they are set up with a Strategy Mindset – with lots of research and outside expertise brought in to help with the process.

What makes an in-house hire work?

Hiring in-house marketers is often successful when a business is of a size that it can hire an experienced digital marketing manager or director to run a department of at least four to five staff – in other words, when it has a spend on digital marketing well in excess of £100,000. At this level, the business is approaching a point where it might be of interest to the better digital marketers in the area, particularly if the business is already on a good growth curve.

But, with the right structure and support, a small business can begin to build its own in-house digital team by combining forces with experienced third parties. Usually this is achieved by hiring one or two content producers, or social media or marketing executives, to work within a broader structure whereby contractors or agencies deliver the strategic and more specialist skills the campaigns need. The third party will often help design and manage the strategy, and also help develop the skills of the staff who are working in house, so that the in-house team can be stable and successful.

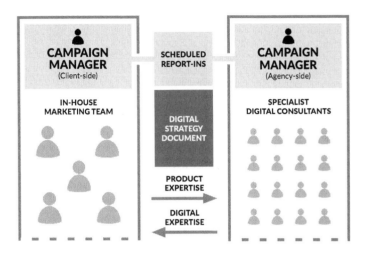

Figure 16 Successful client–agency relationship structure

The structure shown in Figure 16 enables smaller in-house teams to simulate the resources and performance of much larger teams because it meets the needs of both the business and its hires:

- In a small business, hires are not likely to be the most experienced digital marketers in the area but they will have aspirations to grow their careers and find a good career path. Being part of a team that is dovetailed with a great agency meets their need to progress through knowledge transfer and ongoing exposure to seasoned experts and bigger campaigns.

- This in turn meets the needs of the business in that its investment in in-house marketers becomes more stable and more likely to deliver good returns.

The staff it hires have more access to best practice and the opportunity to build their skillset more quickly, which in turn has an impact on the results they deliver. Staff turnover slows so the business gets on average 3 years instead of 1 year from each hire, thereby reducing the cost and disruption of re-hiring.

- This structure also brings continuity and accountability that benefits the business. The right external party serves as the guardian of the business's digital strategy, assisting with re-hires when needed, flagging when internal work is taking the business in the wrong direction and advising on further hires that will be needed for the next phases of growth. Regular dialogue between campaign leaders on either side of the relationship assists this, which is why face-to-face reporting at least once a month is so important.

Whether hiring our first in-house marketers with a view to building a small team or growing our in-house team to five to ten full-time specialist digital staff, we still need to make the right hires. But because most businesses don't specialise in hiring and managing digital marketers, many make poor decisions that set them back on their growth paths. So it works to involve other more experienced stakeholders in hiring decisions and also, of course, to ask the right questions at the application and interview stage.

Questions to ask when hiring in-house marketers

1. What examples can you show of when you generated great returns for other businesses? What numbers did you achieve for them? How did you get those results?

2. There are lots of great agencies in the area and lots of big corporates with in-house marketing departments. Why do you want to progress your digital career with us?

3. Digital marketing is a broad discipline that requires lots of different personality types and skillsets. If you were only going to be responsible for one area of our digital marketing, what would it be?

4. How long have you spent on average with each of your previous employers? What is the shortest and longest period you've spent with anybody? How long do you plan to be with us?

5. If you join us, a likely goal would be for you to deliver X leads/sales from [digital channel] within [number of months]. What would you need from us to deliver this goal?

6. Tell us about your learning patterns. What books have you read in the last six months? Which

experts do you follow on YouTube and social media? What have you learned from them?

7. If you were to join our team and deliver results for us, what other skillsets would you need around you so that you could grow, develop and succeed with us?

2.3

Hiring Contractors And Freelancers

Some digital marketing experts choose not to work in agency or in-house teams, preferring instead to offer their services as independent contractors. In-house contractors are attractive to larger businesses such as corporates who run fixed-term projects. It works better for them to assemble the right people to deliver their short-term projects at higher day rates than to have lots of experienced staff on payroll if demand for them may fluctuate.

In these larger team environments, contractors who have a history of delivering on similar objectives previously are usually hired. When a specialist recruitment agency is involved in the process, they have an interest in vetting and providing staff who are known to be able to deliver on objectives. Companies may hire and re-hire the same contractor several times over. So there are several ways in which the risk of hiring somebody to deliver a particular result for a business can be managed.

Conversely, in environments where a small business is not so experienced in hiring digital marketing contractors or freelancers, the risk is high. This is particularly so because, as we've established, the barrier to entry to present as a digital marketing practitioner is relatively low. So businesses are prone to falling into the trap of hiring somebody who appears convincing rather than somebody who is properly vetted. Just as with in-house hires, the wrong contractor hire can kill growth for a long period. It can be several months before a business realises what's happening, and it can take just as long to unravel and rectify poor work.

Motivations for working as a contractor or freelancer
. . . .

If we're considering adding a contractor or freelancer to our team, before we begin speaking to candidates it's useful to consider the different motivations people have for working outside agency or in-house team environments. Digital marketing experts take this path for credible and legitimate reasons, but there are also people who take the independent route because they have struggled to establish themselves in team situations.

On identifying the need for a particular skill for its campaigns, a business might use websites such as Upwork, People Per Hour or LinkedIn to search for somebody working independently who presents as having the relevant expertise. When we meet and interview candidates on this basis, it's useful to be aware of three reasons that lead people to list themselves as available to work independently, rather than in full-time employment, as part of a settled and established team:

- For some, the motivation centres on a desire for a particular lifestyle – for example, they feel a need to work more flexible hours or that they would like to control more carefully the type of work they do. The reality of working independently is very different, of course, and it is difficult to control demand as a freelancer or contractor. But the motivation is straightforward, and when there is the right match all parties can win.

- Some might be in full-time work but making slower progress up the career ladder than they would like, so advertising as a freelancer provides a means of topping up their income with 'side projects'. Because this type of freelancer is not fully focused on their work for their employer or their freelance projects, they don't fully succeed in either area. They are under time pressures in both environments and don't give full attention to either.

- Others have personality types that have led them to struggle in team environments. This may be to do with their ability to work in a team or because they have not mastered their discipline sufficiently and colleagues or employers have eventually challenged them on that fact. Unable to hold down a good position in a team environment, they switch to presenting as a freelancer or contractor for opportunities where accountability can be lower. Clearly it's important to filter out those who match this profile when interviewing to build a digital team.

Of the three groups, the first is obviously the one to hire while the others are to identify at interview stage and avoid. People who are contracting or freelancing because of a genuine motivation around lifestyle can be great assets to a small business: they can be both skilled and loyal. A useful indicator of this type of person is a career history with stints several years long with credible employers – genuine industry experience. They were respected and retained when they were in employment and there is a good chance they'll be respected and retained when working independently too.

Motivations for hiring a contractor or freelancer

We have some insight into the motivations of different types of contractors and freelancers, but why might a business look to hire an individual rather than an agency? With the Strategy Mindset, our aim is to assemble the most skilled and experienced people to deliver our strategy, so our motivation in hiring an individual should be that they are the option most likely to deliver the result we are seeking.

In high-growth environments, the cost of expertise is normally outweighed by the expected returns. A contractor or freelancer will likely cost more per day than an in-house recruit, but less per day than an agency. But all hiring decisions have to be commercial decisions. A £100 saving a day on any hire may feel good on the day the hiring decision is made. But a £100,000 swing either way in returns at the end of the campaign is a more significant figure. So hiring decisions should always be made on the basis of which approach we consider will give us the best results and returns.

Whether a business is likely to scale up and dominate its sector online if it relies on individual contractors or freelancers is another question. Let's consider the upsides and downsides of this option.

Four upsides of hiring contractors and freelancers

1. There are contractors and freelancers who are skilled and experienced, and who have moved to working independently after successful careers purely for lifestyle reasons.

2. When a contractor or freelancer can bring a niche skill that is needed for one element of a business's strategy, they may genuinely be the best person for the job.

3. A contractor or freelancer will often work without a long-term contract so it's easy to remove them from campaigns if they are not delivering.

4. In cases where a good match is found, a contractor or freelancer can become dependent on work from the business and, as a result, can be bought in and loyal.

Four downsides of hiring contractors and freelancers

1. Contractors and freelancers have finite capacity but demand for their services fluctuates. Pressure on their time may have an impact on the level of engagement, and the results and returns we see from them.

2. If they become ill, overbooked or disappear, our campaigns are suddenly left under-resourced, which has an impact on results and can take time to resolve.

3. Relying on an individual can mean that key information about our business and campaigns resides in their head rather than in our business.

4. A contractor or freelancer may see us as a priority initially but, if a bigger or better-paying opportunity comes along later, we may become less of a priority for them.

If we think back to how great teams are assembled in other areas of working life, the best people are sought and organised into a sustainable structure that delivers predictable results. Part of that structure is about accountability and face-to-face reporting. We want the simplest team structure possible with the fewest lines of communication. When we hire, we should therefore think not only about whom to hire but also about the simplest possible structure that will work, and within which one can communicate with one another effectively.

Questions to ask when hiring contractors and freelancers

1. Digital marketers are normally strong in some areas but not all. If we were to assign you to just one area of our campaigns, which should it be?

2. What case studies and examples of work can you show when you have personally delivered big results for businesses that are similar in size or sector to ours?

3. Why have you chosen to work as a contractor or freelancer rather than in an agency or in-house team where you might learn so much more over time?

4. In the last 12 months, what is the busiest you have been in any given week and what is the quietest you have been? What do you do when you are overbooked?

5. How many people have you worked for in the last 12 months? And how many are you still working for today?

6. When and from where would you prefer to deliver your work for our campaigns? How much

time would you want to spend with us face to face to deliver results?

7. A goal we might assign to you would be to deliver X leads/sales from [digital channel] within [number of months]. What would you need from us to deliver this and how long would it take you to do so?

2.4
Hiring Digital Agencies

When a business is using digital to scale up or dominate its sector, a digital agency is usually one part of its digital delivery team. This is even true of larger businesses with nine-figure turnovers. Businesses of this size may have large in-house teams, perhaps fifty people or more. But digital agencies are usually retained for the mix of expertise they bring, and for their up-to-date knowledge of what is and isn't working across a range of channels and sectors.

Despite this requirement, what we tend to see is marketing managers and marketing executives who are frustrated with their digital agency. They often say things like 'We're not really sure what they do', 'They don't really bring us any new ideas' or 'They're slow in getting back to us.'

These are simply signs that the wrong digital agency has been hired, or a good agency has been hired but one (or both) of the parties isn't managing the relationship effectively. Hiring a digital agency and making the relationship work requires many of the same principles we apply when we hire in-house staff. We should vet them properly, set clear expectations, maintain face-to-face reporting, and review and adjust regularly to keep everything on track.

Here we'll consider some factors that increase the chances of making the right digital agency hire, and of making the relationship effective once the hire is done. To begin, let's look at the different types of agency there are so that we can shortlist appropriately.

Three types of digital agency

Remember that it pays to keep our structure as lean and simple as possible, with the fewest possible lines of communication. So, in some cases, multiple agencies might be needed but where possible we are aiming to hire just one. Before we can begin the hiring process, we need to be aware of the three different types of agency that exist in the market:

- **Full service agency.** Full service marketing agencies provide all aspects of marketing including digital, and also usually including brand development, design for print, exhibitions and PR. These tend to be the bigger agencies and all the services are available under one roof. There is great convenience in this but obviously the trade-off is that full service agencies do not usually live and breathe digital, so the results and services they can deliver for businesses are unlikely to match those of a specialist digital agency.

- **Digital agency.** Like full service agencies, digital agencies provide a mixture of services and bring experience of delivering digital marketing for many different clients. The difference is that all the staff in a digital agency are specialists in digital marketing. Services are likely to be a mixture of promotion or optimisation services (e.g. SEO, PPC, conversion rate optimisation, content marketing and social media) and web production services (e.g. design, build and maintenance of digital assets). For these reasons, where results from digital are vital to a business, a digital agency is usually hired.

- **Niche agency.** Some digital agencies choose to become specialist in a particular niche of digital marketing rather than providing the full range of services. So, for example, some niche agencies provide promotion but not production services. Others might specialise only in niches that are valued by high-end e-commerce businesses such as conversion optimisation or usability testing. Sometimes digital agencies subcontract niche agencies on larger projects and other times they are hired in directly by clients.

Once we have an idea of which type of digital agency is most appropriate to help us deliver the goals we've set, the process of finding the one that is best matched to us begins. Just as with staff, poorly matched client–agency relationships fail and eat up lots of time and budget in the process. Conversations with potential agency partners are more productive when we're clear on what their motivations are likely to be, so let's consider that next.

Behind the scenes at the agency

If we were to ask a hundred digital agency owners about their favourite client relationships, they would all be able to list some that are particularly special to them – special, perhaps, because the fit is so good, the relationship is so strong, everything works for both parties, there's a real openness, results are consistently delivered and the account is profitable too of course.

But most will also have client relationships that are the opposite, where the retainer is ticking along, not quite delivering, communication is difficult, goalposts seem to keep changing, decisions are taken without the agency's involvement and, as a result, the agency feels powerless to deliver growth for the client in question.

For both the agency and the client, the first relationship here probably feels like one that's worth investing time in. It's the one where it pays to go the extra mile when there is the chance to do so, because it feels like a relationship for the long term. The second relationship feels like one that will come to an end one way or the other. The agency seeks to service it by the book, but naturally puts its best resources on the accounts that have the best long-term potential.

A bought-in digital agency partner

So it's in our interests not just to hire the right agency but to set up and manage the relationship in a way whereby we make ourselves a priority for that agency. We're looking to set up a win–win relationship in which the agency is the right agency for us and we feel we are the right client for them – one where there is long-term potential for the relationship to work for both parties.

To achieve this, we bring the Strategy Mindset to the hiring process. We base our hiring decision on evidence – for example, a five-minute phone call to three existing clients of that agency adds so much colour to whatever they present to us in their pitch. And when they do pitch, we probe, make sure we ask challenging questions and listen carefully for evidence in their answers.

We should know, for example:

- how many staff the agency has
- how many will be involved in our account
- what the reporting structure internally is
- whom we will deal with day to day
- what results these people have achieved for businesses like ours already

- what budget the agency thinks we should be placing with them, and how that compares with their smallest and largest accounts

- why the agency wants to work with us rather than other businesses that have approached them

We're looking for clarity on whether the agency will be hungry to serve us once we are on board. Do they have everything they need to achieve the result we're seeking? Sure it may feel good in the cool office with the glossy presentation and the (hopefully) nice coffee. But what will be happening after six, twelve and eighteen months? We need to feel confident on that before we commit to a hiring decision, because it can be a lot of work to undo a wrong relationship once it is up and running.

Setting up for success

Once we have made our decision on which agency we want to hire, the way we onboard them will influence how the relationship plays out over time. A good agency will know how to set the relationship up to succeed, but remember this is not a mature sector and many agencies have yet to identify and formalise best practice. Our experience is that setting up a relationship ladder, whereby multiple relationships are maintained (see Figure 17), is most likely to lead to success and to mean that, when an issue does occur, everybody is aware and it is quickly escalated and resolved.

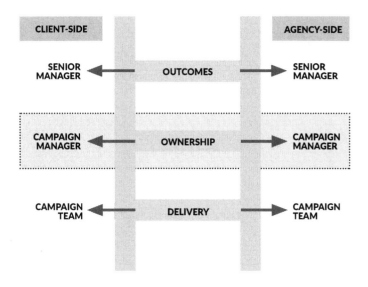

Figure 17 The relationship ladder

With the relationship ladder in place, a fundamental requirement is that the campaign managers meet at least once a month and look each other in the eye as they talk results. For this to work, we need other aspects of the Strategy Mindset to be firing too. We must have our published strategy handy so we're all clear on what's expected, we must have the rest of our team in place to deliver it, we must have the right digital assets and our daily routines must be up and running. When all these aspects are in place and working, we have the chance to scale up and dominate our sector online.

Questions to ask when hiring digital agencies

1. What examples can you show of when you have achieved big returns for businesses similar to ours? Are you happy for us to call those clients for a reference?

2. How many staff do you have? What is the structure? Which are your biggest and smallest departments? Which are the most and least heavily booked?

3. How many clients do you have on your books and how many do you meet with every month to discuss the results you've achieved for them?

4. What are your own plans for the next 12 months? Who will you be hiring and why? Why are we a fit for you in the next 12 months?

5. What would be an appropriate monthly budget given the goals we have? Where would that budget position us in terms of your smallest and largest client accounts?

6. If we do sign with you, who will we deal with on a day-to-day and month-to-month basis? What are their backgrounds and what results have they achieved in their careers?

7. A goal we are likely to set up is to achieve X leads and sales by X deadline from [digital channel]. What would you need from us to achieve this?

2.5

A Winning Team Mentality

So now we know that we're aiming to put together the simplest team structure we can, and we have some ideas now on how to do our hiring well. But what needs to happen day to day for that team to succeed? What does the culture need to look like? And what steps can we take to help our team have a winning mentality from the outset?

Five factors are usually present within a successful digital team – that is, a digital team that consistently delivers the leads and sales needed to scale up a business and dominate its sector online. Some issues are about structure and some are about culture. Hires will usually only work effectively when these five factors are also in play:

1. **Buy-in.** All team members have all been bought into the story behind the campaigns. They have visited the business and recognise the opportunity that exists to grow it. They see this as something they want to achieve for the people behind the business and as a good project for their own careers too. They can see why the campaigns will be meaningful and they believe they can succeed.

2. **Leadership.** Team members know who the leader of the campaigns is and believe that they have the knowledge and experience needed to achieve the result. They respect the leader's judgement and the direction they want to take. They like the

leader and want to deliver for them, and they feel the leader likes them and will reward them for successes achieved.

3. **Ownership.** Each team member understands clearly the area they are responsible for. Their goals are clear and measurable so there is no ambiguity about whether they are achieving them or not. So, for example, if somebody is responsible for paid search, the number of leads or sales required and the cost per acquisition are clear. This way, they always know whether or not they are on track.

4. **Face-to-face meetings.** All team members meet face to face at least once a month to report on their individual results. This happens even when there is an awareness already of some of the results. Team members know they need to prepare and present their outcomes clearly. They know they also need to show why they expect to be delivering their goal successfully next month too.

5. **Visible progress.** Team members feel progress as it is happening. It may be numerical – for example, they can see how their part of the campaign is feeding success in the campaign overall. Or it may be that we feed back directly when we see success. The team then feels it is building something, and that its mission is succeeding, and team members become increasingly bought in the more results are achieved.

Things don't always go completely to plan though and within reason that has to be accepted. So what happens when things aren't quite working? How do we know when to make changes?

Making changes
. . . .

Results are not always predictable in digital marketing. Campaigns play out in constantly evolving marketplaces. Competitors change tactics, Google changes algorithms and audiences shift to new social channels. A skilled and experienced team can adapt relatively quickly when it needs to. But what do we do when we have a dip in results that has gone on for some time?

In the 'Goals And Roles' chapter in Part One, we saw how supporting goals feed an overall goal. When reporting is clear, we can see easily when one or two tactics are failing and then isolate the cause. It isn't always so straightforward of course, but there are some questions we can ask when we aren't seeing the results we expected:

1. **Do we have the right tactics in place?** Could it be we're looking to the wrong channel to achieve results? It's unlikely we've made a wrong call if we had skilled and experienced people choosing the goal. But in 'Choose Your Tactics' in Part One we marked some tactics as 'reserve' and

this might be the time to call on them. It could be, for example, that our PPC is great but our landing page conversion rates are poor. We need to identify that and make changes and, if we've appointed well, the leader of our campaigns will have the expertise to make that call.

2. **Do we have the right people delivering each tactic?** When we know a tactic can work successfully in our market (perhaps because it has worked for us before or because we know it is working for a competitor), we then have to look at who is delivering that tactic for us. Do they actually have the skill and experience required to manage that tactic? Maybe there is a training need? Maybe we made the wrong hire? The Strategy Mindset is about having the best people for each role so, if we need to bring in somebody stronger, the leader of our campaigns has to make that move.

3. **Are our goals and budgets realistic?** If we chose what we thought were sensible goals and sensible budgets with no historical data to work with, it might be we need to switch around some of our supporting goals. Maybe organic search isn't going to deliver the results we anticipated, but maybe paid search can overperform? Our research should have led us to set realistic goals and budgets but if we made a mistake we must identify it and adapt our goals and roles accordingly.

The primary goal doesn't change. Supporting goals can change, tactics can change and people delivering them can change. But the primary goal is the reason we have the strategy – it's the endpoint. Where we are going doesn't change, but how we get there might.

Think of it like a car engine. It's a long journey and we may have to replace or service one or two of the parts along the way. But we don't put in a whole new engine or decide we're only going to go part of the way. We do a quick roadside fix when we hit a problem, confirm we're good to go again, put the final destination back in the satnav and push on until we get there.

TEAM SCORECARD

Businesses that dominate their sector online are usually strong in all four elements of the S-T-A-R formula. Score yourself on the team element by allocating points to each of the ten statements below, based on the following scoring system:

2 = very true, 1 = partly true, 0 = not true.

We feel certain we have appointed the best digital agency partner for us.	2	1	0
We know that senior management are pleased with our performance online.	2	1	0
Our in-house team regularly engage with outside parties for training.	2	1	0
Our digital marketing skills are stronger than those of competitors.	2	1	0
Everybody in our digital team knows the goal they are responsible for.	2	1	0
We have an agreed leads/sales goal with our digital agency partner.	2	1	0
Our in-house team is managed by an experienced marketing professional.	2	1	0
We feel we have all the skills we need to dominate our sector online.	2	1	0
When our digital team reports in, the goals we have set are normally met.	2	1	0
We sit face to face with our digital agency partner at least once a month.	2	1	0

Add up your total to see which band your business is in.

16–20: In the context of your team, you're working with a Strategy Mindset.

10–15: You've lots still to put in place before you'll scale up predictably, but you've made some progress.

0–9: This is a low score, but most businesses have low scores. Will yours be the one that steps up and improves?

Take the full test and get your business's digital strategy score at:

https://getmyscore.digital

PART THREE
ASSETS

Build Your Assets

Earlier we learned how organisations adopt the Strategy Mindset when achieving a particular outcome is vital. Then we went on to look at how we can make digital campaigns deliver predictable results by bringing a strategic approach to them too. But, like those big organisations, we need great assets in place too for our digital team to be able to deliver our strategy successfully.

We saw that professional sports teams with the best players and training facilities are more likely to dominate. In the corporate world, organisations with great branding, facilities and products are the leaders in their markets. And the military understands that it needs the best equipment and intelligence in place for its campaigns to have the best chance of succeeding.

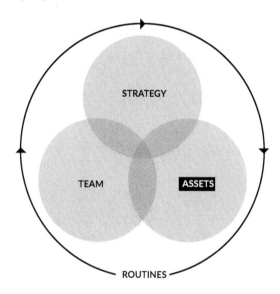

Figure 18 The S-T-A-R formula

Take these assets away and even the big players in these areas would soon struggle. It's the same for our digital team. We can have a great strategy and great people but, unless we equip them with good digital assets, it is difficult for them to succeed.

The third aspect of the S-T-A-R formula is assets (see Figure 18), and in our case that means *digital* assets. It's rare that a business dominates its sector online without great digital assets, and it will become even more rare as digital continues to mature. Whether it's insights, branding, content, websites or data, it's no coincidence that the best performers are usually those with the best digital assets in place.

In this section, we focus on the most common digital assets the leaders in each sector online normally have, and we share tips on how to develop them to a high standard and get the most from them.

Five types of digital assets

We can think of digital assets as being like the foundations of a building. Without them, everything else is unstable and likely eventually to fall over. Campaigns have less chance to succeed when digital assets are poor and, when they are successful, it's by chance and not likely to be sustainable.

Five types of digital asset are usually in place when a business is scaling up or dominating its sector online:

- **Insight assets:** Documented research and insights that give us deep understanding of our customer, our competitors and our positioning.

- **Brand assets:** These enable us to present ourselves correctly and consistently regardless of who is running our digital campaigns.

- **Content assets:** These mean we can quickly and frequently publish content that builds rather than dilutes our brand equity.

- **Website assets:** Great website assets mean that when our target buyer is ready to engage with us it is quick and easy to do so.

- **Data assets:** A by-product of our campaigns is data, which only becomes valuable when we organise, maintain and use it well.

It's not enough just to have each type of asset in place – quality is important too. The creation of some assets is usually outsourced because an in-house team rarely has the skillsets needed to deliver all the assets themselves. Some also benefit from a third-party, neutral approach (insight assets, for example). But, regardless of how they're produced, we must have good digital assets in place if our campaigns are to succeed consistently.

Digital assets as investments

Building great assets isn't just about the impact they have on current campaigns. They're described as 'assets' because they add value to our business and pay dividends in the long term. As we invest in them, we invest in our business. Some impact our bottom line immediately while others assist campaigns incrementally over a period of time, either by reducing the time involved in creating each campaign or by increasing the returns they deliver.

Great digital assets add value to a business in three ways:

Multiplier effects. Each marketing campaign we run has a cost. The cost is made up of the value of our time, any direct advertising costs (such as pay-per-click fees), and overheads such as the cost of our premises. With great digital assets in place, we not only reduce set-up costs (e.g. by having quick access to branding, images or customer insights), but we also increase the likely return our campaigns will deliver because we give them a better chance of being right first time.

Bottom-line effects. Some digital assets have a direct impact on our bottom line. For example, investing in unique custom-built websites, CRM (customer relation management) systems, and CMS (content management systems) serves our business needs and can enable us to claim tax credits for research and development in some cases. Also, when we develop our own systems, insights, branding and content in a structured manner, our business becomes more interesting and more valuable to both potential investors and buyers.

Knock-on effects. As well as direct benefits, many digital assets can have positive knock-on effects too. They can keep our digital learning in the business itself rather than in the head of an employee or contractor – a library of documented research and insights, for example, or centralised and segmented prospect or customer data. Having digital assets readily available also reduces friction for our marketing team, making their day-to-day work more enjoyable and more productive, and means it's easy for incoming staff, agencies or contractors to deliver great work quickly.

So it works to think of digital assets as investments that can pay dividends many times over once the initial work is done to put them in place. And without them our campaigns will struggle to be as strong as those of the leaders in our sector online. That's why we call them 'assets'.

Building a library of assets

If we think of the Strategy Mindset and how large organisations approach mission-critical campaigns, usually the full range of required assets is made available. That might be intelligence, data, systems, facilities and equipment – mature organisations recognise the need for the right tools to be in place. And when they recognise a need or gap in what's available to their teams, they take swift steps to address it.

As we build our digital assets, the same should apply. It doesn't work to have great customer insights but poor branding, a great CRM system with poor data in it, a great website but lead magnets that don't appeal to our target buyer. The business that dominates each sector has a full suite of well-developed digital assets, stress-tested through being in use on a daily basis.

Figure 19 shows the five different types of digital assets and some common examples of each. These lists aren't exhaustive, and what's required will vary from business to business, but sector leaders will usually have most of these in place.

So if our intention is to scale up, and perhaps even to dominate our sector online, our business needs to quickly develop these digital assets to a high standard. We will now look at each type of asset in greater detail.

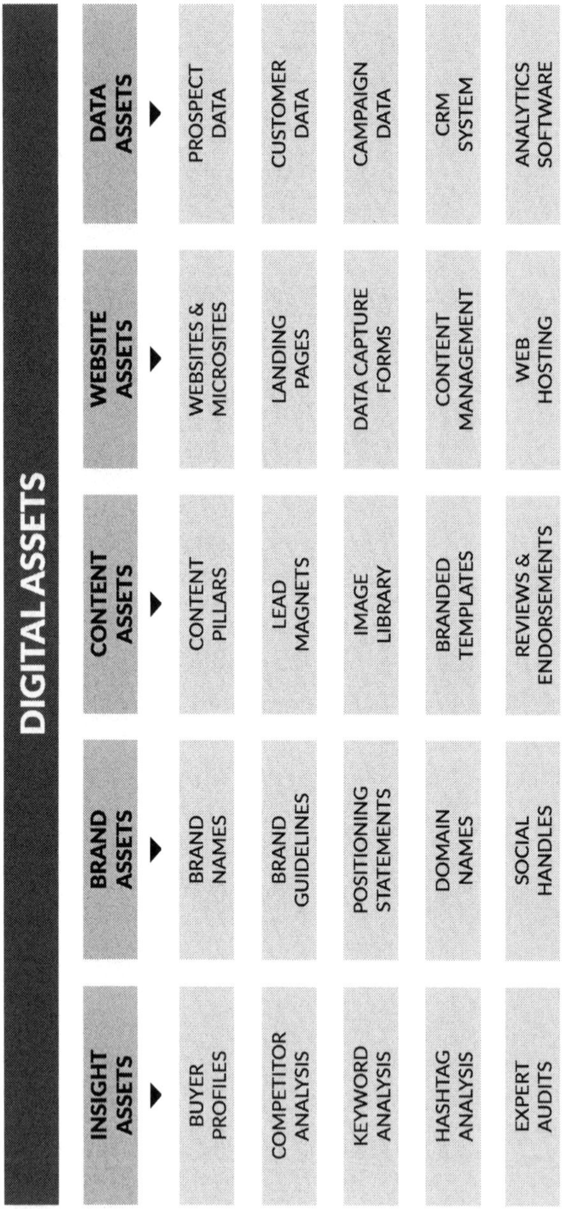

DIGITAL ASSETS				
INSIGHT ASSETS ▶	**BRAND ASSETS** ▶	**CONTENT ASSETS** ▶	**WEBSITE ASSETS** ▶	**DATA ASSETS** ▶
BUYER PROFILES	BRAND NAMES	CONTENT PILLARS	WEBSITES & MICROSITES	PROSPECT DATA
COMPETITOR ANALYSIS	BRAND GUIDELINES	LEAD MAGNETS	LANDING PAGES	CUSTOMER DATA
KEYWORD ANALYSIS	POSITIONING STATEMENTS	IMAGE LIBRARY	DATA CAPTURE FORMS	CAMPAIGN DATA
HASHTAG ANALYSIS	DOMAIN NAMES	BRANDED TEMPLATES	CONTENT MANAGEMENT	CRM SYSTEM
EXPERT AUDITS	SOCIAL HANDLES	REVIEWS & ENDORSEMENTS	WEB HOSTING	ANALYTICS SOFTWARE

Figure 19 Digital asset types

3.1
Insight Assets

A trait that differentiates those with the Strategy Mindset from those with a Lottery Mindset, Agency Mindset or DIY Mindset is that decisions are made based on research, data and insight rather than on whims. So it follows that, to achieve the predictable results the Strategy Mindset brings, we must first build up those insights within our business.

Once we've carried out thorough research on our customers, competitors and the marketplace we operate in, the insights we have can pay dividends many times over. If we file them and make them available for colleagues, they can fuel future campaigns by enabling our team to save time and achieve more predictable results. We learn so much when we deliver digital campaigns that it makes sense to bank our learning so that it can benefit our campaigns in the months and years that follow.

It's best practice then to build and maintain a library of insight assets that our team can refer to as they plan and roll out our digital campaigns. It's for each business to decide how much time and budget it should invest in each of its insight assets. But as a minimum we should have a deep understanding of our customers, competitors and marketplace. To get us started, here are some of the main insight assets digital teams with the Strategy Mindset are likely to have in place:

Buyer profiles

In 'Know Your Customer' in Part One, we learned that, if we're to produce marketing that resonates with our target buyer, we must first understand their pain points. We have to know what truly matters to them. It may be there is more than one target buyer to consider – for example, one person may be the target for the product but another may control the budget and approve the purchase. In such cases, our team should develop a good buyer profile for each. Our buyer profiles should live in a central location for our digital team to refer to on a daily basis as they deliver campaigns. When digital marketing loses that focus on its target customers, campaigns cease to connect and deliver to their full potential. Buyer profiles help our team to retain that focus.

Competitor analysis

Equally important is our focus on competitors. Competitors can become out of sight and out of mind for a digital team, but our target buyer has them front and centre as they make buying decisions so we have to be clear on how our marketing differentiates us from them. Competitors are constantly evolving themselves of course, so reviewing the market and updating competitor analysis documents is a recurring task – quarterly or six-monthly depending on how quickly our sector moves. As with buyer profiles, competitor analyses should be on hand for our digital team so they can quickly recap how to build campaigns that will make us stand out in a crowded marketplace.

Keyword analysis

Professionally researched keyword analysis helps us create content that is matched to the language in our buyer's head, and the search terms they use. Often the terminology we use in our businesses is different from that used by the target buyer. This is because the buyer is seeking to solve a problem and so searches the problem, while we are thinking of selling our product or service as solutions so refer to those instead. Good keyword analysis sense-checks assumptions on language, terminology and search volumes, and provides groups of keywords around which we can build content and optimise our paid, organic, social and email campaigns.

Hashtag analysis

Audiences have shifted somewhat in recent years from organic search to social spaces and it's usual now for target buyers to follow or search for partic-ular hashtags in major social channels such as Twitter, Instagram and LinkedIn. Hashtags also dictate which profiles are suggested to users of these channels, so we have to know what the most popular hashtags in our sector are. Tools such as hashtagify.me help us understand hashtag volumes, and social campaigns should then be planned around the hashtags most commonly used by our target buyer. This doesn't just increase the visibility of our posts – it also grows our audience, which increases our credibility online both for our target buyer and for Google.

Expert audits

It's possible to carry out our own digital audits, but it often pays to have independent experts review the fundamental aspects of our digital footprint from time to time. As well as an unbiased perspective, this gives us the chance to gather knowledge by exposing our team to a third party's approach to assessing our digital assets and campaigns. Expert audits that are commonly outsourced would include website audits, SEO audits, PPC audits, CRO audits and social media audits. A good audit includes both quantitative and qualitative analyses, shows understanding of our customers, competitors and the marketplace we operate in, and includes prioritised recommendations we can action straightaway that will directly improve the performance of our campaigns.

3.2
Brand Assets

The strength of our online brand obviously has a major bearing on the results our digital marketing can achieve. If we ask our team to do their best work and equip them with a brand that doesn't align well with our positioning, we limit the results they can achieve. Businesses that are scaling up online and dominating their sectors have simple, memorable and appropriate branding that enhances their campaigns by giving users clues about the values and positioning of the business before they even read or consume any content. When we think of those we regard as leaders in a sector, we can usually immediately picture their branding.

When we have strong branding and promote it, we build brand equity. So how strong is our brand? What proportion of our target buyers already instantly recognise us? Do the majority know us and perceive us as we would like? Can they understand our values and positioning when they first see a piece of our marketing? Or are we a new brand with work to do to build recognition among our target buyers?

In digital marketing, starting out with a strong brand benefits us in two ways. It means the marketing work we do reinforces an already successful brand. And it means our marketing efforts are likely to yield better returns because our branding is strong. Great brand assets enable our team to deliver these two benefits. Here are some of the digital assets strategy-minded teams have in place to help them consistently deliver successful campaigns:

Brand names

Our online brand often goes beyond our company name. Many businesses develop multiple online brands, and sometimes they have brand names for particular products or services. Think of Apple and the iPhone, both now established as strong brands in part because they are always presented consistently in terms of spelling, capitalisation and typeface. Customers know the iPhone brand so well the product is often marketed and searched for on that one word alone. We're not all as big as Apple, but we can develop clear and memorable online brand names and product names within our own marketplaces. When search is important, a distinctive name can help us dominate organic and social channels too. Again, big players have done this – Google, for example, runs no risk of being confused with anybody else. So it works to develop consistent brand and product names, and to document how they should be presented so that our digital team can promote them consistently.

Brand guidelines

Brand name conventions are usually clarified in a brand guidelines document, and these documents contain much more besides. The purpose of a set of brand guidelines is to enable marketers to present an organisation consistently regardless of who delivers the marketing. They show, for example, how our logo is used in different situations, which fonts can be used, what type of images are appropriate, what our colour palette is, and often what example brochure and web page layouts look like. Big players present consistently so our being consistent presents us as credible too. As a team follows brand guidelines over time, it builds brand equity. When there are no guidelines and marketing is inconsistent, the more marketing we do, the more we actually erode our brand equity. So it pays to have good brand guidelines in place.

Positioning statements

A good brand assets file is also likely to include tag lines, slogans, mission statements and brand values lists. These enable our marketing team to quickly understand and recap our personality and positioning before they begin work on new campaigns. Some organisations publish their brand values and positioning statements on their websites. This level of openness helps build trust among target buyers, while helping them to understand our offering and positioning more deeply. Because one of the responsibilities of our marketing team is to pitch us correctly to our target buyer, developing good positioning statements and keeping them on file is another key to delivering consistent campaigns.

Domain names

Organisations should have domains for current and potential future brand names and product names registered both for their own use and to prevent others from registering them. Sometimes it's possible through negotiation to retrospectively retrieve a domain name we failed to register, but it's cheaper and easier to make sure that our business owns the names it might need from the outset. New domain name variants are frequently becoming available, such as.tv,.shop,.global and.consulting so it's useful to consider which is most appropriate as our main domain, and which should be registered and redirected to that main domain. Domain names build value and authority, and over time can become respected by Google, resulting in our website ranking improving. Domain names are therefore business assets. A company should keep records of the logins of its domains and make sure that they are registered to the company and not to an employee, to reduce the risk of losing them in the future.

Social handles

As with domain names, our social media handles should be short, snappy and sensible. It's great too if they are consistent across all our social channels. Some users will search our brand name on social channels and these autofill, so a good social handle can make it easy for our target buyer to identify and follow us online. Having the same handle across Twitter, Facebook, Instagram, Snapchat, YouTube and LinkedIn is great if we are lucky enough to be able to register them all. As with domain names, because our social handles are business assets, it's important that they're registered to company social accounts and that records of logins for each exist, rather than their being set up by and registered to individual employees or contractors.

3.3
Content Assets

The most effective digital campaigns are usually run by businesses that have assets in place that enable them to publish great content regularly and consistently. They therefore spend less time producing content than their competitors, and they build clearer understanding among their target buyers about their positioning and offering. Without good content assets, a digital team isn't able to work so efficiently and the chance of inconsistent content being published online increases.

The Scottish craft ale company BrewDog is a good best-practice example. Founded in 2007, they quickly became the UK's fastest growing food and drink company. In part, that's because they publish some of the strongest online content the drinks industry has ever seen. Their brand quickly became familiar to prospects and customers because they promoted the same branding, products and key messages across the main social channels every day. They also back up their advertising with a blog almost every day, built around the same content as their social posts.

Businesses like BrewDog scale up and dominate online because their groundwork is done. Their digital teams are empowered by having great content assets to draw on. They're clear on their content plan, have imagery and branded templates ready to go, and content calendars that make good use of them. So it's quick and easy for them to publish across all channels, and they're consistent and on message across the board, irrespective of who does the work. With such good assets in place, it's actually difficult for them to push out poor content.

Let's take a look at some of the content assets successful digital teams like this would usually have in place:

Content pillars

We'll look at content pillars in a little more detail in Part Four, Routines. They are the core themes we push across all our marketing. They're the themes we have decided speak best to our target buyer's needs and which best define our positioning for them. Content pillars exist as assets when a business publishes long-form content around them. For example, white papers, PDF guides, eBooks, videos, audio interviews and so on are great ways to publish insightful content around the themes most important to our business. It's then easy for other marketing team members to draw on these to publish lots of additional content on various subtopics related to the core content we have invested in.

Lead magnets

Most of our content is intended to build brand awareness or familiarity with particular products or services. But at some point we want prospects to engage in some way too of course. One way to do this is to offer downloadable content and this can be done in the form of lead magnets. A lead magnet is content or functionality that is valuable enough for the prospect to share contact details in return for accessing it. Some common lead magnets are brochures, white papers, free book chapters, PDF guides, interactive scorecards and free webinars. When a prospect engages with a lead magnet, they've taken a positive step to engage with us, so, whether we've collected useful data in the process or not, they are strengthening their relationship with our brand. In this way, it pays to have good lead magnets in place.

Image library

Elsewhere in this book, we've referred to the low barrier to entry in the digital sector, which can lead to poor-quality online marketing being delivered for some businesses. This is the case where imagery is concerned too, because anybody can take photographs with their phone now and stock imagery is readily available too. Imagery, therefore, becomes an area where a business can steal an advantage by building a library of professional on-brand images that can be used throughout its digital campaigns. So, if we show a product, it's properly lit; if we're speaking at an event, we don't show empty chairs; and if we're showing our offices, they're clean, on brand and full of happy, professional-looking staff. A well-organised library of images saves time and ensures a perception of quality and consistency across multiple campaigns.

Branded templates

Earlier in this section we explained how BrewDog delivers daily content across their main social channels and their website, and we explained that it's always all on brand. Their videos, images and graphics all follow exactly the same style, as is usually the case across corporates and sector leaders. Less successful businesses post unbranded or inconsistently branded content. When a business creates a set of templates that match its brand guidelines, it provides its digital team with an easy opportunity to build that same consistency. Branded templates should be always on hand and set up ready in the correct sizes for use across all the main social and paid search channels.

Reviews and endorsements

Trust signals are a key factor in maximising conversion rates online and there are few better ways to build trust than to show our products or services being endorsed by customers who have used them. Keeping a good, up-to-date set of reviews or endorsements on file provides an organisation with an asset it can draw on across any future campaign. Reviews and endorsements might take the form of written testimonials, video testimonials, celebrity endorsements or five-star reviews. Particularly in B2B sectors, businesses that scale up often evidence that their product or service is a good option by showing that those who have committed to purchasing already are pleased enough with the outcome that they have left a review or testimonial.

3.4

Website Assets

Attracting prospects and then converting them to customers online is usually a multi-channel process. But the final conversion still tends to occur on a website or web page of some description. Think back to Google's 7/11/4 concept, which we introduced in the 'Know Your Competitors' chapter in Part One. We surround the target customer so they're aware of us and, when they're ready, we offer them an opportunity to take things a step further and actually engage with us. Because that engagement happens on a web page more often than not, the quality of our website assets is key in enabling our campaigns to deliver on their goals for leads or sales.

So, usually the businesses that scale up and dominate their sectors have the best website assets. But it isn't just our target customer that is interested in who has the best website, Google is interested too and will make us more or less visible in search rankings depending on what signals it picks up about the quality of our website and its content.

Off-the-shelf systems such as WordPress and Magento are common and there are many good examples of these – and, because of their ubiquity and ease of access, many bad examples too. In most sectors, the biggest players are not using these off-the-shelf systems and Google knows that. They are working with layouts and code that have been carefully crafted around enterprise-level coding frameworks or CMSs to deliver the best user experience and fastest load times of any competitor. This more bespoke approach, when done well, delivers better results and better rankings.

When the Strategy Mindset is not in play, a website is a box to be ticked – if it is in place, decent and fairly new, it's 'job done'. In high-performance environments, it's a vital business asset, just like premises or staff. The organisation has recognised that it must have the best website in its sector. In bigger firms, it's common too for there to be multiple websites or landing pages for different target buyers, so that each campaign provides the perfect user experience for the buyer in question. Let's take a look at some of the website assets businesses that scale up and dominate online usually have in place:

Websites and microsites

If structured and promoted well, our main website will build a great reputation in Google and, provided the content within it is professionally curated and produced, it will then rank above competitors too. Google now places prominence on how fast websites are and how well they perform on mobile devices. These factors are so important that Google even provides online tools to score our websites against its criteria. Conversion rates can be increased with the use of microsites for specific products or services, so the user is not distracted by information that isn't relevant to their search. Google can tell if a website is a low-budget templated system or a custom-designed high-end website based on a coding framework, and it knows that big players usually have the latter.

Landing pages

For short-term campaigns, specific product or service offerings, or new ideas we are testing, it often works well to send prospects to specific custom-made landing pages rather than to our main website. Main websites often contain information on lots of topics so have to be carefully structured to convert visitors before they become distracted. A landing page is a standalone page on a single topic that has just one purpose. Usually that purpose is to give the relevant information on a specific topic or question and to invite an enquiry or purchase. Landing pages are quick and easy to set up either through our website CMS (a good CMS will have the facility to create them) or through third-party systems such as Leadpages or Unbounce. Standalone landing pages aren't designed to rank well in search engines so traffic is usually sent via paid ads and landing pages are removed when campaigns end.

Data capture forms

Many websites fail to perform because their CTAs are overly complex, with more friction than necessary for the target buyer. CTAs include enquiry forms, mailing list sign-up forms, buttons to download white papers or brochures, or a shopping basket. They are literally the parts of the website that call our visitors to take some action. Once we have sensible CTAs in place, we can test them by changing wording a little or by changing their size, colour or location on the page. Tracking results of such changes helps maximise the performance of CTAs, which in turn maximises the results we see from our campaigns. As we would expect, the most successful companies in each sector online have forms that are tested and refined, and which perform somewhere close to their full potential.

Content management system

Campaigns that deliver high growth usually involve regular publishing of useful and interesting content. For this to be successful, a digital team needs flexibility in how it publishes content to its websites. We should be able to vary our page layouts a little, and to add rich elements such as images, videos and perhaps forms and interactive tools where appropriate too. The flexibility, reliability and ease of use of our content management system (CMS) is therefore a key digital asset. A good CMS minimises the time we spend working on campaigns and helps our team to build new pages that are fast, well optimised for mobile devices, and that rank well in search engines. Without a good CMS it's difficult for our campaigns to succeed.

Web hosting

Although perhaps not immediately obvious, the way we host our website has a significant impact on how

Google and our prospects perceive us. We know speed is an important ranking factor for Google and we know it has an impact on conversion rates. Google can tell whether our website is running on low-budget hosting or on professionally configured cloud or dedicated servers. Businesses that dominate their sectors have websites that not only look the part but are also fast and easy to use. Our choice of web hosting directly affects all these factors so premium-grade hosting is a key digital asset for a business that is serious about scaling up and dominating its sector online.

3.5

Data
Assets

A valuable by-product of marketing campaigns is the data they generate. Each time we log a new prospect or customer, we create the opportunity to share value with that person or company for months or even years to come. So the data we accumulate from our marketing activity can scale up over time and the biggest returns on it may actually come some way down the line. Despite this, many businesses just accumulate and sit on data until it becomes too outdated to be of any real value, rather than nurturing it so it can be used to its full potential.

Maintaining data means quality checking it over time and keeping it appropriately segmented and up to date as we collect new information about each prospect. Just as a garden needs weeding to avoid it becoming unmanageable, our data needs to be looked after and kept in good order too. When an organisation is maximising the value of its data, it keeps on top of duplicates, updates customers' contact details and makes sure that the prospects and customers on its databases are genuine target buyers of the organisation's products or services.

In the European Union, businesses now have to comply with the General Data Protection Regulation (GDPR). This means that we must:

• track how we accumulate our customer data

- make sure that we have each person's permission to hold it (or there must be a mutual legitimate interest in our holding it)

- provide an easy opportunity for people to have their data deleted

- notify the regulator immediately in the event of a data breach

Our campaigns, products and services must therefore provide enough value for prospects to feel they want to allow us to hold their details and to communicate with them from time to time. The following are some examples of data assets that help us to deliver valuable content to the prospects and customers we are seeking to build relationships with:

Prospect data

The GDPR will likely mean a trend away from the practice of buying email lists and marketing en masse to them. In its place, organisations will likely carry out marketing activity to accumulate interested prospects by offering valuable content in return for their interest. So sign-up forms will become more common, as will free valuable content such as white papers, PDF guides, scorecards and other lead magnets. There are advantages to these approaches, most notably that, done well, they will leave businesses with better-quality data to work with than bought-in marketing lists ever will. They will result in much more engaged prospect databases.

Customer data

Once prospects come on board as paying customers, they begin providing us with even more useful data. They're now buying our products or services so they can be segmented by product or service type, frequency of purchase, average spend and so on. We can target emails, display ads or personalised content at the most appropriate times for them, and with the most appropriate messages and offers. For example, if somebody is buying products for 0–3-month-old babies, we have a good idea what they might be thinking about buying in 3, 6 and 12 months' time. By managing our data well, we're able to offer more valuable content to prospects and customers, which leads to campaigns delivering greater returns too of course.

Campaign data

Each time we run a campaign, we learn how our audience reacts. So the more campaigns we run, the more we build understanding about their behaviour. To bank this learning, we can reflect on our campaigns and file our learning for future reference so that we can shortcut to successful approaches in the future (see the 'Reflect' chapter in Part Four for more on this). By way of example, each time we run a paid search campaign, we gather understanding of what went well and what didn't. This data is an asset because it enables us to run our paid campaigns well straightaway next time. A good marketing manager will record results and make past learning easily available to the broader digital team on a day-to-day basis.

Customer relationship management

Prospect and customer data becomes more valuable if we manage and log activity against each contact in a customer relationship management (CRM) system. CRM systems can be set up to automatically log everybody who gets in touch with us – for example, when they complete a form, make a purchase through our website or even visit a particular web page. Our CRM can then track our activity with each customer – for example, by enabling us to log notes on conversations we've had with them. Based on these, we might decide, for example, that a particular segment of customers should go into a fast-track marketing campaign, and that others should go into a nurture campaign. A good CRM enables us to segment and plan, and to run such campaigns quickly and easily.

Analytics software

As our website and social channels run, they record data on who finds our content and on how they engage with it. Google Analytics is the most widely used platform and most websites use it to record activity. But other software is available and social channels also return analytics data. Analytics helps us understand things like the location, demographics and often even the intent of the groups of users who visit different parts of our websites and social channels. But analytics software is only valuable when it is set up well and we have expert analysis of the data it returns. Once configured correctly, our analytics software becomes an asset because it provides a steady stream of data that helps us to run increasingly effective marketing campaigns over time.

ASSETS SCORECARD

Businesses that dominate their sector online are usually strong in all four elements of the S-T-A-R formula. Score yourself on the assets element by allocating points to each of the ten statements below, based on the following scoring system:

2 = very true, 1 = partly true, 0 = not true.

We have a brand guidelines document that our digital team uses.	2	1	0
We own all the domain names and social media handles we need.	2	1	0
We know that our website(s) score well on Google Mobile Friendly Tests.	2	1	0
Our social channels have been professionally branded and optimised.	2	1	0
We have professionally produced photography and video available.	2	1	0
We know that our website(s) score well on Google Speed Tests.	2	1	0
We use marketing automation to manage and filter the audiences we build.	2	1	0
We have spent more than £10,000 on our website(s) in the last two years.	2	1	0
Our website delivers the quantity and quality of leads we need it to.	2	1	0
Our website has been overhauled or rebuilt in the last two years.	2	1	0

Add up your total to see which band your business is in.

16–20: In the context of your assets, you're working with a Strategy Mindset.

10–15: You've lots still to put in place before you'll scale up predictably, but you've made some progress.

0–9: This is a low score, but most businesses have low scores. Will yours be the one that steps up and improves?

Take the full test and get your business's digital strategy score at:

https://getmyscore.digital

PART FOUR
ROUTINES

Build Your Routines

Much of the S-T-A-R formula is about set-up and preparation. It's about laying foundations so that our digital team can be consistently productive and can deliver campaigns that are predictable and profitable.

The fourth and final step, Routines, is different (see Figure 20). Our daily, weekly and monthly routines are when we capitalise on the groundwork we did by developing our strategy, assembling the best possible team and building great digital assets. We capitalise by publishing and promoting daily content, and by reacting to feedback from prospects as they receive that content. We make ourselves more visible than others. We put ourselves in front of prospects and command their attention.

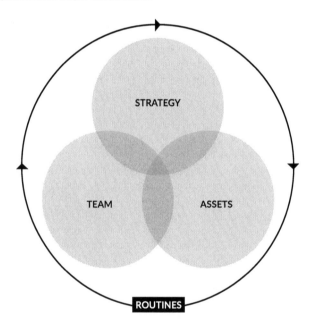

Figure 20 The S-T-A-R formula

Notice how marketing routines run in cycles around our strategy, team and assets, which are constants. The routines we set up will enable us to continually improve those constants – the strategy, team and assets – because the more good marketing routines we have, the more we learn, and the more we learn the more we are able to fine-tune the foundations our marketing team has in place.

Learning from best practice

We've seen already how large organisations operate with the Strategy Mindset to put great strategies, teams and assets in place. But they don't win just because of that preparation. They win because they execute well too. They consistently deliver, they reflect and they bank their learning by documenting what they have found to be best practice, so that future team members can also deliver great marketing.

They don't let their strategy slip from focus and become preoccupied with peripheral marketing activities that aren't supporting the organisation's core objectives. They don't work like busy fools on a day-to-day basis on campaigns that nobody is sure are working. And they don't jump between marketing ideas on whims, never executing any properly. Yet over two decades in digital, this is how we see most small businesses running their digital marketing.

We see, for example, businesses repeatedly publishing content that gets little or no engagement. We see them publish content that isn't centred on well-researched content pillars, or that is of a quality that is eroding the business's brand equity rather than strengthening it. We see businesses hiring staff on whims because they've heard a particular type of digital marketing can work – they want to feel somebody is busy doing something about digital, whatever it is. And we regularly meet businesses that have little idea whether or not they are getting a return on their investment in digital marketing.

The Strategy Mindset is about bringing a structured approach to digital marketing – and that means in our day-to-day work too. So daily routines are run as bigger organisations would run and review their campaigns – strategically and with scheduled reports and reviews. This enables us to keep costs under control and to understand exactly what is and isn't working so that we can refine campaigns accordingly as we go along, and constantly improve results.

Campaign thinking

The most effective digital teams think of marketing as campaigns rather than an ongoing endless process. Campaigns have start and end dates, they have focus among those involved in delivery, they usually have easy-to-measure costs and returns, and their fixed-term nature provides an opportunity to capture learning and record a tangible outcome on completion (see Figure 21). This learning becomes an asset to help future campaigns run more effectively.

Campaign thinking enables teams to earn recognition for successes quickly. A sold-out event, sign-up targets achieved, leads and sales targets hit or costs reduced on long-standing campaigns are some examples of how a digital team can win the confidence of peers within an organisation. The more successes a team registers, the more trust in it builds, the more the team is valued, and the more it is rewarded and invested in by the organisation.

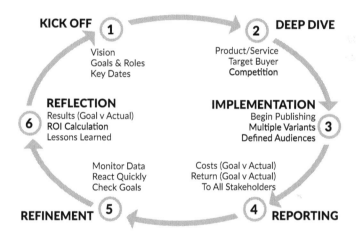

Figure 21 A digital campaign cycle

Some digital campaigns run regularly, while others are one-offs. Some have predictable results because they are variants of those that have been run before. And some are experiments, perhaps to test a new product or service idea, or to test a new approach to marketing. But all have focus, are measurable and provide returns, whether financially or in terms of learning – or, as is often the case, both.

Moving towards predictable outcomes

· ·

The S-T-A-R formula, when implemented thoroughly, is a self-fulfilling prophecy in that its four components feed one another once they are up and running:

- Our **strategy** is based on deep insights into customers and competitors. As we deliver campaigns, we learn more and build deeper insights for the future.

- Our **team** should have the right skills and structure. As we deliver campaigns, we build skills and make changes when we aren't seeing results, and our team strengthens.

- Our **assets** must be implemented well across the board. When we deliver campaigns, we grow and improve our digital assets as we work with them on a day-to-day basis.

- Our **routines** succeed if we have a solid strategy, a great team and the right digital assets. The three constant elements enable us to deliver our routines efficiently and effectively.

So using digital to scale up our business and dominate our sector online is about preparation across our strategy, team and assets, but also about good execution of daily, weekly and monthly marketing routines. In this section, we will look at the three types of marketing routines – Recycle, Refine and Reflect – and we'll consider what they look like when they are being delivered well.

4.1
Recycle

One of the things that separates those who dominate their sectors online and those who don't is the extent to which they exploit content after they create it. By way of example, a business might spend half a day creating a piece of content and then share it two or three times across a couple of social channels. Because social posts have a short lifespan, the chance of the target buyer finding it are slim and the chance of them engaging with it are even slimmer.

Businesses become the most visible in their sector when they build lots of genuinely valuable content to start with and then effectively add a multiplier to its impact by exploiting it many times over. They recycle content over weeks, months and in some cases even years to make sure that they surround their target buyer with their messages. And when they've taken care to make sure that their content speaks to their target buyer's pain points, the target buyer remains interested and engaged.

So what does it look like to recycle content on a daily, weekly and monthly basis? And which types of content are easily recyclable and which are not? Once we know, we can invest time in the areas that will bear most fruit over time. Remember that the extent to which we exploit our content determines how visible we are in our particular market, so it pays to plan and deliver genuinely valuable content that can be used over and over again.

What are content pillars?

Content pillars are core themes that speak to our target buyer's pain points. They're the handful of topics we speak about repeatedly in our marketing. Usually a business has a blend of a few content pillars that, when combined, position it clearly to the target buyer. So for example, a construction firm might establish three content pillars as follows:

1. A record of on-time and on-budget projects (40%)

2. Real-life project examples in target sectors (40%)

3. A commitment to environmentally friendly projects (20%)

The percentages indicate the ratio of content the business wants to publish on each of its three pillars. With the themes of its pillars established, it becomes easy for the business to produce content around them. For example, for the first, there might be a leaflet on the principles the company follows that make its projects successful. For the second, there might be a library of online case studies that they add to each month. And for the third, perhaps a white paper on why construction projects can and should be environmentally friendly.

The beauty of content pillars is that the business invests in creating them once but, because they are longer-form content, they make it easy for colleagues to produce on-message and on-brand content around them. If we have a white paper, we can pull out subtopics from it and produce perhaps ten blogs, fifty social posts, three video explainers and an infographic. Our one piece of core work is then exploited exponentially. By repeating this approach, we can become the most visible business in our sector.

With established content pillars, if we add new staff, freelancers or agencies to our team, all can refer to those pillars and build subtopic content quickly and easily. Content stays on brand and on message. Establishing the ratio of content we should produce on each helps keep our messaging balanced. In the construction company example we used earlier, it wouldn't work for the company to spend 80% of its time talking about environmentally friendly projects with no evidence of them completing projects successfully. But the right combination of content pillars, in sensible ratios, gives a marketing team an easy-to-understand formula for producing and recycling lots of on-brand content over time.

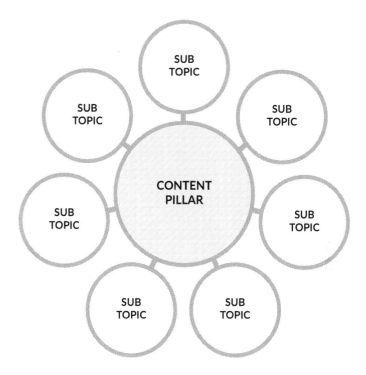

Figure 22 Content pillars and subtopic clusters

Good content pillars can be exploited far beyond the website on which they are published. We can build whole microsites around content pillars (see Figure 22). We can build social campaigns, blog content, email campaigns, video and audio content, and interactive tools around the themes we've established. The most visible online businesses invest in strong content pillars and then employ skilled digital teams to exploit them over and over again on a daily, weekly and monthly basis. That's why they become the most visible businesses in their sectors.

What is evergreen content?

• •

We can take recycling of content a level further by making sure that plenty of what we publish is evergreen content (see Figure 23). By 'evergreen', we mean content that doesn't go out of date, that we can recycle over long periods of time and that we might still be sharing and benefiting from a year or more after it is produced.

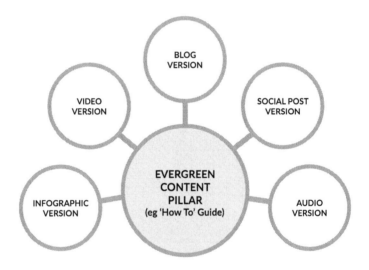

Figure 23 Recycling evergreen content

When we produce evergreen content, we increase the return on investment (ROI) of that marketing activity because we aren't just relying on an immediate short-term win. A business can produce evergreen content in January, republish it throughout the year in different forms and potentially win leads from it every week of that year. So when we produce content calendars and content plans, it's sensible to consider how many times we can rerun particular content or even whole campaigns. It works to over-compensate with repeating content – while we might be aware of everything we put out, our target buyer is likely to be only seeing and engaging with a small percentage of it.

Some examples of evergreen online marketing content are:

1. **'How to' guides.** In some sectors, target buyers search for instructions or 'how to' guides to help them make progress with their problems. When these are fundamental issues, they generally don't date quickly, so guides can be republished many times over across different platforms.

2. **Case studies.** We know that target buyers look for evidence to prove that we're able to resolve their issues. Case studies provide that proof and once the components are assembled (as text, images and video, perhaps) they can then be recycled across different online channels over time.

3. **Infographics.** For our marketing to work, our target buyer must recognise that we understand the issues they are trying to make progress with. Infographics relating to our content pillars can usually be recycled many times, and with

infographics what's even better is that, if they're good, our audience will do lots of the sharing for us.

4. **Video footage.** Accumulating good-quality video footage – for example of interviews, instructional demos and events we have run – is valuable. These can be rerun, recut and repackaged in many different ways. Video around our content pillars is particularly valuable because it gets lots of engagement on many different channels.

5. **Reviews and testimonials.** Most businesses recognise that it's good to gather reviews and testimonials, but how many fully exploit these once they have them on file? When we assemble a library of endorsement graphics, they can be recycled regularly across our campaigns. Repetition of these reinforces trust in our brand among our target buyers.

The 7/11/4 concept

When we think about how to recycle our content, it's useful to remember Google's theory (introduced in the 'Know Your Competitors' chapter in Part One) that prospects need seven hours of content over eleven touchpoints across at least four channels before they reach the zero moment of truth, when they feel ready to buy from us.

Most prospects only see and engage with a small proportion of the content we publish, so we should always overcompensate with the amount we publish. Recycling content across different platforms over time is the most efficient way to do that. When that recycled content is based around carefully planned content pillars, we build brand equity over time and also give ourselves the chance to be the most visible supplier in our sector online.

4.2
Refine

A vital element of successful digital marketing is optimisation and refinement once campaigns are up and running. This mirrors the Strategy Mindset approach that more mature organisations bring to other areas of their business. They don't work blindly or with a finger in the air – they analyse and seek marginal gains wherever they can achieve them.

In digital marketing, there are differences between how sector leaders behave once campaigns are running and how those who usually find themselves playing catch-up behave. The differences are in how they monitor and refine campaigns. Businesses with Lottery, Agency and DIY Mindsets tend to adopt a fingers-crossed approach whereby, once a campaign goes live, it is considered done and they simply hope that good results will follow.

But big players become big players because they have a mentality of continual refinement. They have an appetite to fully understand their audiences and to react to feedback as it comes in from their live campaigns. Their strategic approach to planning and preparation means that they regularly land close to the perfect campaign to begin with. But they then make sure that their campaigns are truly great by monitoring the response as they run and by making adjustments based on what they learn.

Incremental improvements are transformative

Refining live campaigns normally leads to what feel like very small improvements. They can be so small that it's not always possible for individual members of a digital team to appreciate the impact their work is having. Actually, becoming the leader in a sector is often about achieving marginal gains across a broad range of metrics. And the more developed a sector becomes, the more marginal gains are what is needed to win, because the bar is already set high.

Let's consider a scenario in which a new campaign has been launched to generate sign-ups to a training course. The profit on each sign-up is £1,000 and the digital team is assigned a set advertising budget to deliver a goal of at least 150 sign-ups. How does the digital marketing team approach the process of launching and refining the campaign so that it delivers that number?

When a campaign is running – successfully or otherwise – there are things we can do to improve performance (more on those options later). But on first review it might feel insurmountable to think, for example, that we can double performance simply by refining small elements of the campaign. And, if we present doubling performance as an objective to our digital team, they may feel it's an unrealistic goal.

Also, as buy-in is usually needed to deliver great results, we run the risk of demotivating our team to some degree.

Alternatively, if we task individual members of our digital team with the responsibility to improve their specific area by just a small amount, the goals we are setting often start to feel realistic. What if the conversion rate at each stage is currently 20% and we brief the relevant team member with increasing it to 25% by the end of the month? Let's take a look at how such marginal gains can have an impact on campaign performance overall.

	DAY 1	DAY 30	WHAT CHANGED?
VISITORS	10,000	10,000	(At fixed budget of £1 per click)
DOWNLOADS	2,000 (CR=20%)	2,500 (CR=25%)	Sam trialled 5 ad variations and found the best one increased the conversion rate from 20% to 25%
ENQUIRIES	400 (CR=20%)	625 (CR=25%)	Joanne introduced a sign-up deadline to her email campaign and saw conversion rate grow to 25%
SIGN UPS	80 (CR=20%)	156 (CR=25%)	Michael noted recurring queries in sales calls and dealt with them in a video FAQ on the sign-up page

Figure 24 How incremental improvements combine for big wins

So in this example three team members each achieved a small increase in performance in their area of the campaign. But their three improvements combined meant the overall campaign performance doubled and the revenue generated grew by £76,000 – a good return from relatively marginal gains across three specific parts of a campaign.

This level of micro-refinement is exactly how those who dominate their sector online reach a point when they're delivering results that are greater than those of their competitors. Their campaigns return far more per pound spent than their competitors' and that's why they're the ones who are scaling up as a result of their marketing activity across digital channels, while others are improving at a much slower pace and are therefore always playing catch-up.

Ways to refine campaigns

Each business and each campaign is unique, and the more skill and experience a digital team has the more easily they are able to identify go-to areas to test and refine to improve performance. Some examples that are common to many campaigns, and that often represent good starting points for refining performance, are as follows:

Audience

First and foremost, is our campaign targeted at the most appropriate audience? If we are using paid search, how accurately have we targeted our campaign? What happens if we adjust the keywords and interests we are targeting? What happens if we narrow or widen the geographical area we are targeting? What happens if we target via different devices or at different times of day? Testing variations removes guesswork and brings certainty on which audience profiles work best.

Ad variations

What we perceive as the perfect ad is often not the one our audience regard as perfect and respond to. Even in a small paid ad, there are many aspects we can refine to improve results. What happens if we:

- try different headlines?
- include or exclude pricing?
- build in a time-limited offer?
- try different types of image?
- try a video instead of an image?
- try different wording on buttons?

Split testing across these and other variables means our audience tell us which ad format connects with them the most.

Automation

Many campaigns rely on a degree of nurturing before there is a transaction. Often that nurturing is in the form of automated email follow-ups, or automated remarketing ads that remind the target buyer of their interest in our product or service. But what does the most effective automation follow-up look like? If we're using email, how many emails should there be? What should the messaging be? How frequently should they be sent? And when is the right moment to invite the target buyer to go ahead and engage with us?

Landing pages

Some campaigns are intended to drive an immediate transaction or enquiry. For example, LinkedIn and Facebook now enable the target buyer to make their enquiry directly within an ad, without visiting the business's website. But more commonly a campaign will encourage a target buyer towards a landing page that:

- provides details and benefits of the product or service

- answers the most commonly asked questions about it

- provides an opportunity for them to enquire or make a purchase

But what layout gets the best result? What content gets the best result? What imagery works the best? What branding? How much detail does the target buyer need?

Calls to action

However we want our target buyer to interact with us, there is almost always some kind of call to action involved. It may be as simple as an invite to phone or email us, or a form to fill out to express an interest, make a purchase or complete a download. The positioning on the page, wording and layout of such forms can have a huge impact on the results we see from our campaigns. There is software to track where users drop out of forms, and eye-tracking and mouse-tracking software can also help us understand where there might be friction for our target buyer. As we become aware of friction and eliminate it, we increase campaign performance.

Short- and long-term wins

Setting up routines to test and improve campaigns provides the opportunity for performance to improve in the short term. And we've seen how marginal gains across different aspects of a campaign multiply to deliver larger improvements in overall performance. But the more we test and the more we refine, the more we gather insight into our target buyer's habits, behaviour and preferences. And the more we learn about the people we are trying to connect with, the better the results of the campaigns we design and implement for them in the future will be.

4.3
Reflect

Businesses with the Strategy Mindset value continual improvement and enjoy building assets for their business, including insight assets, which gather together accumulated knowledge and research. We learn the most from our campaigns when we stop at the end to reflect on them, because we then have the chance to understand why each campaign performed as it did. Stopping to reflect enables us to capture learning, and over time the process effectively finetunes our understanding of what best practice is.

The reflection stage is a skill in itself and the better at it we become, the more substantially our campaign delivery improves over time. Even when a campaign has delivered successfully, it may be that we can identify areas where we could have reduced costs, involved fewer people or delivered even greater results – or perhaps ideas arose along the way for related campaigns that we feel could also be successful. When campaigns end, our job is to bank learning so it is quickly accessible for our current team and for others who may run our campaigns in the future.

We learned in Part Three how accumulating great digital assets helps a business's digital marketing perform better over time. When documented and logged well, the learning we can accumulate from each campaign becomes a business asset that can be referred to many times in the future. In this section, we share a process for reflecting on digital campaigns after they have been delivered, and for logging our learning in a way that will benefit our business over a long period of time.

Five-step campaign review session

. . . .

1. **Recap goals.** Sometimes campaigns are short and smooth and other times they're long and noisy. For example, in a twelve-week campaign, we may recognise the need to change course after a couple of weeks and then change again further down the line based on results. In larger teams, or teams where leadership is not so strong, focus on the proposed approach, and in some cases the campaign goals themselves, can become diluted and understood differently by some team members. So the first step in a campaign review is always for the campaign team to sit together and recap the goals they had set. And of course we can't review how our campaign performed without being clear what it was supposed to deliver, so some questions to ask are:

   • What goals was the campaign intended to deliver?

   • What did we decide upfront about how we would achieve them?

   • What did we agree about the costs and resources to be allocated?

2. **Create a campaign timeline.** Different members of a campaign team may also have different interpretations about how a campaign played out. That's because campaigns usually include people with different areas of expertise, and one aspect might have run smoothly while another

chopped and changed several times to achieve its result. How well the project team communicated during delivery influences how much of a shared understanding they have of how the campaign as a whole went. It helps in a reflection session to map out the sequence of events from start to end (usually on a whiteboard or large sheet of paper) so that the discussion is based on a shared understanding of what happened during the campaign. Creating this kind of visual timeline also helps identify where lessons were learned. Some questions to ask are:

- What were the start and end dates of the campaign?

- What were the key events during the delivery timeline?

- At what points did we learn things during the campaign timeline?

3. **Calculate ROI.** To be successful in marketing – digital or otherwise – we usually have to be delivering good returns on the campaigns we run. It's the only reason we're hired as marketers and, if we run campaigns that don't deliver good returns, eventually people stop hiring us. So a fundamental for any marketer is to be able to accurately show the ROI of any campaign or project they've run. It's a simple calculation but important to get right, because showing correct numbers gives stakeholders confidence in us – it shows them we care about their costs

and whether their spend with us is paying off or not. The difference between profit generated and revenue generated is key. It is the profit that pays for our marketing activity, not the revenue, so marketers should always be reporting back the margin achieved on any leads or sales, rather than the total value of them. If we don't have exact data for profit, it is best to agree a typical margin with our client and use that for the calculation.

$$\text{ROI} = \frac{\textbf{PROFIT GENERATED} - \textbf{CAMPAIGN COST}}{\textbf{CAMPAIGN COST}} \times 100$$

Figure 25 Calculating return on investment

This is the normal formula for calculating return on investment and it gives the result as a percentage, so no sales will always show a result of –100%, and when the profit is double the campaign costs it will always show as 100%. A break-even project will show 0% ROI. Some questions to ask after calculating the ROI on our campaign are:

- What profit did our campaign generate?
- What was the total advertising spend of the campaign?
- What other campaign fees or staff/time costs were incurred?

4. **The Four Ls.** The first three steps of this session give us the context we need to have a productive reflection session, and they help team members begin to share their observations. But, because our aim is to log learning so that other team members can positively influence the outcome of future campaigns, the chair must set an appropriate tone. There should be a constructive discussion focused on taking responsibility for campaign outcomes. The Four Ls is a common format for gathering ideas for lessons learned. Headings are posted on the wall in four categories: Liked, Learned, Lacked, Longed For. Each team member is invited to write their comments for each on a post-it note. Then, one by one, they read out their ideas and stick them in the relevant section. Some questions to ask during this step are:

- Which lessons will help us deliver better campaigns?

- Which lessons can we most easily act on?

- Which is our biggest learning from this campaign?

5. **Lessons-learned logs.** With ideas for learning posted on the wall, the chair facilitates debate on which of the lessons might enable the team to improve performance most in the future. Similar post-its are grouped into themes to simplify the discussion, and they're marked as most or least valuable in terms of how they might help future campaigns. By the end, the campaign team

should have a clear sense of what the biggest takeaways from the project are. The chair then records those in a log for future campaign teams to refer to, as in the following examples:

- How would we best categorise our learning for future teams to use?

- Are there lessons we can share with colleagues right away?

- Which is our favourite lesson learned from this campaign?

Building a lessons-learned log

Campaign reviews benefit businesses most when lessons are logged centrally in a way that makes them easy to access in the future. A simple spreadsheet where lessons are tagged with themes is all that is needed (see Figure 25). The log can be referred to any time and even be filtered to just show learning we have recorded for particular types of campaign.

For example, if a team is planning a new paid social campaign, it's helpful for them to be able to quickly review the company's learning from past paid social campaigns. The lessons-learned log shouldn't include duplicate entries, just new lessons. It is useful, however, to note if a lesson has come up more than once in a reflection session because that is then a flag that the digital team needs to give more focus to it to stop it from recurring.

CAMPAIGN TYPE	LESSON LEARNED	LESSON TAGS	LOGGED BY
Workshops Lead Gen	15% conv. uplift with authentic rather than stock event photos	Facebook Ads	Connor March 2018
Scorecard Completions	Better matched leads from AdWords than Facebook	AdWords, Facebook Ads	Chris March 2018
Workshops Lead Gen	30% more enquiries when CTA is to register for news on dates	Facebook Ads, CTA	Lauren April 2018
Workshops Lead Gen	Video of delegates post-event saw conv. rate increase 12%	Landing Pages, Video	Bethany May 2018
Digital Exec Recruitment	'Register Your Interest' 2x as many responses as 'Apply Now'	Social Promo, CTA	Mel May 2018
Scorecard Completions	More click-throughs when described as '4-minute test'	Facebook Ads	Amanda June 2018

Figure 26 Example of a lessons-learned log

Lessons can result from wins as well as failures of course, and some lessons may be general and may apply to all campaigns. For example, 'having a weekly review where everybody reported their number saw performance increase' is a very broad lesson. It's the job of the chair to help the team identify what they delivered well and what contributed to achieving goals, as well as where their work could have been better. With this kind of process, the accumulation of learning adds up to a bank of knowledge that becomes an asset to the business because it helps future campaigns shortcut to successful approaches, which minimises wasted spend and increases returns.

Marginal gains

• • • • • • • • • • • •

Much of what we have described in this Part Four is about marginal gains, and the more saturated and competitive the digital space becomes, the more marginal gains are how people grow to dominate their sectors. These activities align us with the culture of the larger organisations we described at the beginning of this book, in which the Strategy Mindset is in play and leading them to continual and predictable success. In the Conclusion, we'll take a look at what happens when we practise digital marketing with the Strategy Mindset over a long period of time, both in terms of what it means for the businesses we work for and of what it means for our own careers.

ROUTINES SCORECARD

Businesses that dominate their sector online are usually strong in all four elements of the S-T-A-R formula. Score yourself on the routines element by allocating points to each of the ten statements below, based on the following scoring system:

2 = very true, 1 = partly true, 0 = not true.

Our website is continually analysed and amended to improve conversion rates.	2	1	0
We have several pieces of evergreen content that continually generate leads.	2	1	0
When we post on social media we normally get more than ten likes or comments.	2	1	0
We publish content to a mixture of social media channels every day.	2	1	0
A prospect could search for us on any digital channel and find great content.	2	1	0
We continually measure how visible we are online compared with competitors.	2	1	0
Our digital team hold a reflection session each time a digital campaigns ends.	2	1	0
Our digital team attend at least five training events per year.	2	1	0
We know our cost-per-lead on each of the digital marketing channels we use.	2	1	0
What we publish online matches our prospect's biggest ambitions or pain points.	2	1	0

Add up your total to see which band your business is in.

16–20: In the context of your routines, you're working with a Strategy Mindset.

10–15: You've lots still to put in place before you'll scale up predictably, but you've made some progress.

0–9: This is a low score, but most businesses have low scores. Will yours be the one that steps up and improves?

Take the full test and get your business's digital strategy score at:

https://getmyscore.digital

Conclusion

The Mastery Mindset

We began this book by considering the different mindsets businesses bring to their digital marketing. We learned that most businesses don't yet have a fully developed approach to digital campaigns. And we then learned how to adopt the Strategy Mindset to create the opportunity for a business to outperform its competitors online.

There was also a fifth mindset, which we haven't yet looked at in any great detail. So let's conclude by considering how some digital marketers are able to graduate beyond the Strategy Mindset towards the Mastery Mindset, and what it means for the businesses they work for, and their careers, when they do so.

The journey to mastery

Malcolm Gladwell popularised the theory that to become world class in any field people must practise their skill for 10,000 hours. The specifics of this theory and the number have been debated at length since, but the principles that practice results in learning and that mastery can't be achieved without lots of practice over a long period of time are not questioned.

Many years earlier, Martin Broadwell published his 'Four stages of competence' theory (Figure 27). This illustrates the steps from being unaware of our

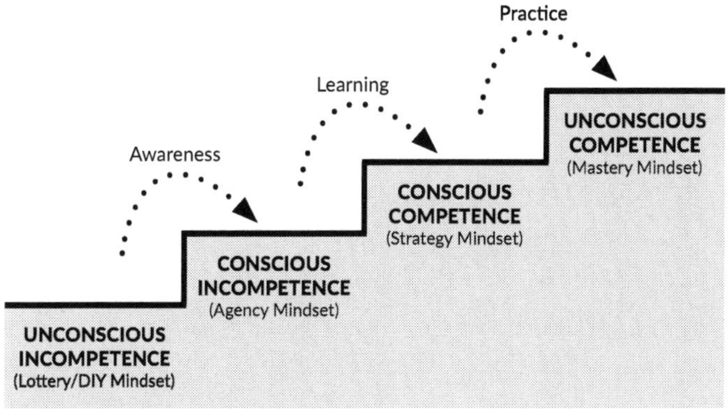

Figure 27 Four stages of competence

incompetence, through realising we need to build skills, through being aware that we have learned, to our understanding being intuitive. These four stages align with the five mindsets of digital marketing in this book, as shown in Figure 28.

The Mastery Mindset is only achieved once we have practised the Strategy Mindset successfully for a long period of time. Crucially, it isn't achieved by simply spending a lot of time in digital marketing. It's achieved by spending a lot of time delivering successful, predictable digital marketing over and over again. This book describes the Strategy Mindset whereby marketing is delivered in a structured manner where there is a culture of refinement and reflection, which enables learning as we deliver.

We probably don't quite need to spend 10,000 hours to achieve mastery with this approach, but we will

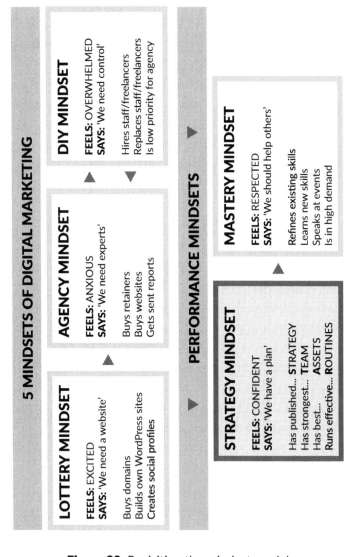

Figure 28 Revisiting the mindset model

need to build years of experience of best practice delivery across different types of campaign. While that may feel a way off for some of us, the good news is there are plenty of rewards for those who get there. Let's take a look at what happens to those who do graduate from the Strategy Mindset to the Mastery Mindset.

Five things that happen with the Mastery Mindset

I'm fortunate that in my day-to-day work I spend lots of time with people who have achieved mastery in digital marketing. I also spend plenty of time with people working towards mastery through our workshops and accelerator programmes. The simple fact that people have reached out to build their knowledge and understanding means that they are on a journey towards more developed mindsets and methods around digital marketing.

I find it interesting that at different stages of the learning journey people tend to say similar things and have similar experiences. Those with the Mastery Mindset have a different demeanour about them. They normally appear relaxed and fulfilled, they enjoy their work and, best of all, they have the time and resources to develop their skills further. They love the subject of digital marketing and it's great to talk to them about it.

Here are five things that happen to people who have achieved the Mastery Mindset in the field of digital marketing:

1. **They're trusted.** Many digital marketers are frustrated that their clients or employers are skeptical about their advice, or don't act on their ideas. They sometimes say they feel held back from making real progress. When we speak to those who have achieved mastery in their approach to digital marketing, they're much more often in situations where they are trusted and listened to. Because they have shown their ability to deliver results repeatedly, their recommendations are taken at face value, and they're trusted with resources and budgets for big and exciting projects.

2. **They're rewarded.** When a team or individual doesn't have a track record of delivering predictable results, there is often some focus on the costs of hiring or employing them. When mastery is achieved, the balance shifts. The laws of supply and demand mean the best people are often coveted by many businesses. The result is the best digital marketers are offered disproportionately good opportunities. They're offered the best packages too – the best remuneration, flexibility, holidays, budgets, autonomy. When we offer mastery, we are more able to choose the terms on which we work.

3. **They speak at events.** Some reach a point where they flip from attending conferences and events to listen and learn to attending to speak and to share their own stories and frameworks. This shift is a clear indicator that mastery has been achieved. It's when somebody's track record is such that others will travel to listen to them, and it's where their experience and understanding are such that they can organise their own thoughts and theories about what best practice looks like. It feels good and it also feeds further development because it means spending time with other digital marketers with the Mastery Mindset.

4. **They keep learning.** One thing that surprises me about those with the Mastery Mindset is that, although they have huge experience, they are often among the most curious and learning-oriented minds in their industry. Perhaps it's because they always had a hunger to learn and that's why they achieved mastery in the first place. Maybe there is something also in that they've seen first hand what a commitment to personal development brings, so they know learning has value and is worth devoting time to. They are often afforded time and budget for learning too, of course.

5. **They love their work.** Perhaps least surprising but most significant is that those with the Mastery Mindset seem to really love their work. They smile, look relaxed and love discussing ideas, campaigns they've been working on and new

developments in digital marketing. And why wouldn't they? They work in a sector that's fast moving and exciting, and they're respected by their peers and recognised as leaders in their field. They appreciate where they are because they remember what it was like to feel overwhelmed by the subject matter, and they feel satisfaction that they're now able to share that knowledge and use it to deliver spectacular results for the businesses that they choose to work for.

Scaling up and dominating a sector online

When mastery is achieved, it isn't just the individual that benefits. When a digital team is led by somebody who has developed the Mastery Mindset, the businesses they work for are usually on exciting growth curves, driven by the results they see from their digital marketing. The more the business relies on leads or sales generated through digital channels, the more this is the case.

This is because the strategy-based approach the person has implemented, and is continually fine-tuning, delivers predictable results for the business. They've established benchmark costs-per-lead or costs-per-sale and are refining them on an ongoing basis. So the businesses they work for not only move towards dominating their sector, but their continual improvement means it is difficult for others to catch them up.

The person's strategy-based approach means they're time efficient too. Because they have built a digital marketing strategy, a great team and great assets, as well as establishing good marketing routines, their campaigns run smoothly and efficiently. So they have plenty of time and headspace to deliver new ideas, and to learn about new digital channels and new techniques. Their degree of mastery continues to grow and the businesses they work for continue to benefit.

Five steps towards the Mastery Mindset

Depending on where you are on your personal journey in digital marketing, it might be that achieving a level that could be described as mastery feels some way off. We've already established it is something that follows years of implementing different types of best-practice campaigns. But progress is achieved through lots of small steps and the occasional big leap too. Take comfort in the fact that most people in your industry don't even bother to buy and read a book like this on digital marketing strategy. The simple fact that you have the mindset to do that, and to work through the book to these final pages, puts you at an advantage.

But real success comes with implementation. Many people feel they could have invented Facebook, but only one person actually did it. Other people feel they could have been on *Top of the Pops*, or could have been a professional sportsperson, but only a small percentage put in the actual work to get there. Anybody can talk about progress but only a small percentage do what it takes to achieve real success. Here are five steps to focus on to progress in your industry and to move towards the Strategy Mindset, and perhaps, ultimately, the Mastery Mindset too:

1. **Implement.** There's plenty in this book that you can do right away (ie, this week). There's a lot you can outsource to get done quickly, too. Once you have built your blueprint – get on and implement it.

2. **Share with colleagues.** It's difficult to make progress in isolation. Let colleagues know about the steps you want to take, and share this book with them so they will understand why.

3. **Enjoy the process.** There will be both successes and failures along the way – that's guaranteed. So enjoy the process as much as the results. All outcomes result in learning and move you closer to the Mastery Mindset.

4. **Celebrate success.** Digital marketing is often delivered with limits on time and budget, so we can feel very busy. Make a habit of noting successes, and of pausing each week to celebrate and appreciate them.

5. **Stay hungry to learn.** Not everybody has hunger to make real progress for themselves and their teams. That gives you the opportunity to stand

out. Be the one who sets the clear vision and puts in the work – be the one who wins.

Enjoy building your digital marketing strategy, enjoy implementing it and as you do feel free to reach out at stevebrennan.co.uk to share your growth journey.

The Author

Steve Brennan has advised over 250 businesses on their digital marketing strategy over a career spanning twenty years. He has helped many through periods of rapid growth online, while simultaneously growing his own digital agency business.

Steve has particular expertise in online lead generation for B2B businesses, and typically works with them through his agency's Digital Accelerator Programme, workshops and events, or on a one-to-one consultancy basis in some cases.

Backed by a team of fifteen digital experts who work alongside him, Steve operates in the UK from offices in Lancashire and London, providing audits and workshops to help businesses make sense of digital, and building high-performing digital strategies, websites and marketing campaigns.

Steve lives in Manchester, England, with his partner and daughter and relaxes by writing songs. He has released three albums with his band Flow Machines – recorded in Manchester and New York – and completed his most recent LP at Abbey Road Studios in London. His music has been featured in the *NME*, *Time Out* and on BBC Radio. He has also remixed or collaborated with several other British bands, including Super Furry Animals, Cornershop, Martin Carr and James.

After twenty years at the coalface in digital marketing Steve is now committed to sharing his expertise with as many people as possible, and to helping the next generation of digital experts at his agency do the same in the decades to come.

Social media

Twitter: @SteveBrennan

Instagram: @flowmachines

Author website: stevebrennan.co.uk

Digital scorecard: getmyscore.digital

Digital agency: bespokedigital.agency

Printed in Great Britain
by Amazon

67925269R00145